WALKS IN DARTMOOR & SOUTH DEVON

Countryside Books' walking guides cover most areas of England and Wales and include the following series:

County Rambles
Walks For Motorists
Exploring Long Distance Paths
Literary Walks
Pub Walks

A complete list is available from the publishers at:
3 Catherine Road, Newbury, Berkshire

WALKS IN DARTMOOR & SOUTH DEVON

Christina Green

———————

COUNTRYSIDE BOOKS
NEWBURY, BERKSHIRE

Originally published as *Walks in Devon* by Spurbooks
This edition, revised and rewalked by the author,
first published in 1993

COUNTRYSIDE BOOKS
3 Catherine Road
Newbury, Berkshire

ISBN 1 85306 162 X

Cover photograph of Widecombe In The Moor taken
by Andy Williams.

Publishers' Note
At the time of publication all footpaths used in these walks were
designated as official footpaths or rights of way, but it should be borne
in mind that diversion orders may be made from time to time.

Although every care has been taken in the preparation of this Guide,
neither the Author nor the Publisher can accept responsibility for
those who stray from the Rights of Way.

Produced through MRM Associates Ltd., Reading
Typeset by Paragon Typesetters, Queensferry, Clwyd
Printed in England by J. W. Arrowsmith Ltd., Bristol

Contents

Introduction

I have chosen 20 walks which I feel show the variety and beauty of the Devonshire landscape. None of them are unduly long or arduous, for I believe the enjoyment lies in the quality of the walk, not merely its length. Personally, I need time to snatch my breath, while I stand and look around, taking in the view, the weather, the wildlife — and letting my mind mull over the spirit of the place. From what my family and friends — who shared the researching of these walks — say, I am not alone in such simple pleasures. So I hope that others will also derive enjoyment from this selection of walks.

The cosiness of Devon's small villages, market towns, river valleys and seaside resorts is thrown into spectacular relief by Dartmoor's remote and sometimes bleak wilderness. Such a varied landscape provides a great source of walking, and I have tried to choose routes illustrating all the aspects of Devon.

A compass is a safeguard and a detailed map of the area is a great source of helpful information. When walking on Dartmoor, in particular, weatherproof gear is essential — the famous mist can come down unexpectedly in just a few seconds, and the bogs hiding beneath the green 'featherbeds' are extremely wet. As I have mentioned elsewhere, if walking in the areas of the artillery ranges on the moor, be sure to find out all relevant information about times of firing before setting out.

At the time of walking my paths were clear and unobstructed, and I hope and believe they will remain so — but, as all walkers know to their cost, weather and obdurate landowners can easily change things. Forewarned is forearmed!

Christina Green
Spring 1993

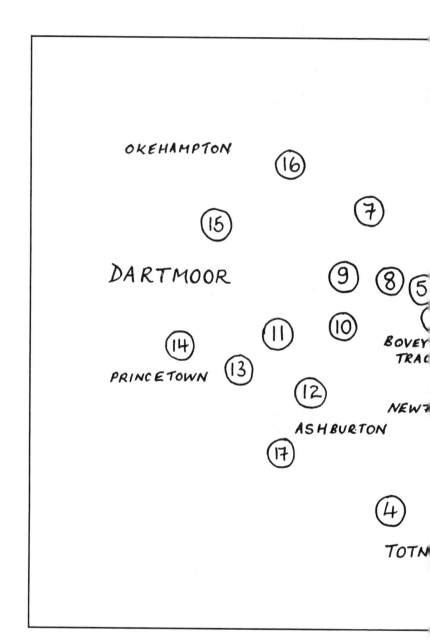

Area map showing location of the walks.

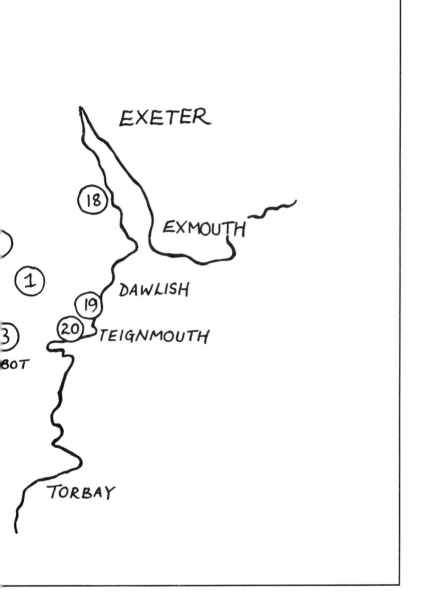

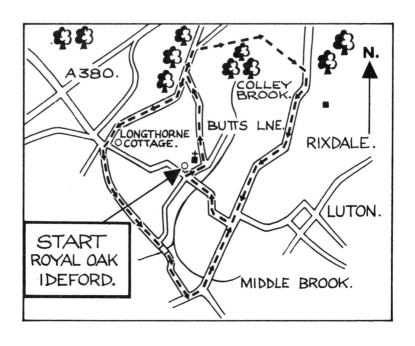

A380.

COLLEY BROOK.

BUTTS LNE.

LONGTHORNE COTTAGE.

RIXDALE.

LUTON.

N.

START
ROYAL OAK
IDEFORD.

MIDDLE BROOK.

Ideford

Three loop walks of 2½ miles, 2½ miles and 3¼ miles.

Half a mile off the humming A380 road to Exeter from Newton Abbot is Ideford, a gem of a rural village. Not obviously spectacular, its picturesque parts are tucked away and must be sought out to be appreciated. It is a splendid centrepiece of medieval paths and packhorse routes, and there is some very pleasant walking to be had through quiet lanes and old bridleways, which may be muddy in bad weather.

The Royal Oak is a good village pub with bar snacks on offer at lunchtime on weekdays only, Monday to Friday. At other times the Elizabethan Inn, ½ mile down the road into the neighbouring village of Luton, has an excellent menu every day.

Cars may be parked on the verge of the road around the Royal Oak and the oak tree which dominates the centre of the village.

Walk on from this point along the road to the left, passing the church, dated between 1300 and 1500. Notice the carved stone fixed to the outside wall of the chancel, which has been dated about 1100 and proves that an earlier Norman church stood on this same site. The stone is a door lintel, depicting a dragon and a pelican, a bird often connected with the early Christian faith. This church had many alterations made to it in the 16th century and again in more recent times. The additions harmonize well with the original stone, as the Red Quarry near Ideford Arch, not far from the main road, provided all the materials.

After passing the church, the road twists left up a hill, but the name of the lane continuing straight on − Butts Lane

— has links with the past, for here, on the fields surrounding the lane, the archery butts were set up for weekly practice.

The hill is a steep one, but has the saving grace of magnificent views from various gateways. These fertile lands, farmed for so many centuries, slope down from the last ridge of the Haldon Hills above. On the left the patchwork of coloured fields runs gently down, leading the eye towards distant Newton Abbot, with the hump of Denbury Camp beyond, and finally to the high curving line of Dartmoor, etched against the sky.

At the top of the hill, notice the ancient trackway running down to the left, full of memories of the Saxon named Ida who came this way, founding the village at the ford down in the valley. Turn left and go down this old road for *loop A* back to the village, passing the 14th century cottage, Longthorne, at the junction of the track with the road, and following the lane slightly to the left on the opposite side of the road. This descends, via uneven, flinty, muddy ground, to a lower road where a barn stands in a wide saucer of rich farmland, and Larcombe Bridge spans the little Colley Brook as it meanders through the fields towards Newton Abbot, where it eventually joins the river Lemon.

The road to the left returns directly to the village, if desired, but *a further loop (B)* may be followed by continuing along the bridlepath, having passed Larcombe Bridge, and keeping to the left at the next fork. This is the old packhorse route to Bishopsteignton and Teignmouth. It joins a hill running down left to a stone bridge and this road, signed to Ideford, brings us to another junction where we turn left again, re-entering the village.

The alternative loop (C), however, from the junction of the hill past the church and the old Saxon track, is to turn right, by the sign 'Ideford Breakers', and then turn right again, following the footpath sign before you reach the Breakers. This track opens out into moorland, bearing left and joining a flint path which runs generally eastwards through Ideford Common. There are magnificent oak trees below, and in these woods, bubbling up through a deep goyle, the Colley Brook rises, falling through fields until it reaches the village and then Larcombe Bridge, crossed on loop B described above.

The flint path continues across the common between heather and self-seeded spruce trees, with one large Scots pine in evidence on the left. This, so legend says, was once used as a gallows and has given the common its name of One Tree Common; the Scots pine may be seen from Hay Tor, a tiny pimple on the straight ridge of Lower Haldon.

If this walk is timed for late afternoon, when the setting sun slips down behind Dartmoor, the colours are unforgettable. In the summer evenings the common is a haven for nightjars, their strange, haunting music filling the silence.

Where the flint track meets the metalled road, turn right and descend the hill, with glimpses of Haldon's high ground to the left. This loop walk is completed by turning right at the signpost at the bottom of the hill — or by cutting off the corner, with the aid of a small footpath crossing a field, and emerging beside two modern houses, on the site of the old village forge, with its history of having been the home of the first grass-cutting machine.

Pass farms and cottages, and spare time to look at some of the old-world and historical names. Ideford has a lot to offer.

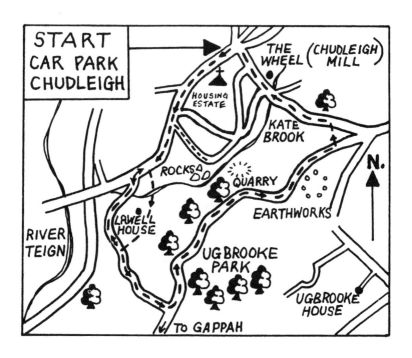

Chudleigh

A 3 mile loop walk with an alternative 4 mile loop walk.

Chudleigh can be reached by bus from Newton Abbot, or by car via the A38 from Exeter. It is a small village where the wheel has turned full circle; the railway has been and gone and Chudleigh today, its traffic banished to the nearby dual carriageway, is quiet and peaceful, once more the 'secret place' of its Saxon origins. Explore the narrow lanes of its surrounding countryside, the relics of past history still evident within the village, and see for yourself what delights Chudleigh has to offer.

There is a large free car park in the centre, with several pubs to afford refreshment. From the car park, Fore Street takes us through a variety of shops and houses to the church of St Martin and St Mary, built originally in 1259. The fire that swept the village in 1807 and destroyed 166 houses spared the church and the Bishop Lacy inn across the road, said to be once connected to the church by a passage. Next door to the church is the old Grammar School, built in 1668. Note the stone in the wall.

Further along the road we make a short but interesting detour, turning left at the police station and passing Palace Farm, built on the site of the Bishop of Exeter's summer palace, dating back to 1080. Through the orchard gate a few fragments of masonry can be seen. There are tales of underground passages and dungeons, and in old excavations, it is said, skeletons were found near the quarry at the end of this road.

Our way takes the unsigned path on the right, entered by an iron kissing gate, which is about 50 metres short of the

Glen Cottage, with its Bed and Breakfast sign, close to the quarry entrance. This path leads upwards to Chudleigh Rocks, a handsome cluster of grey limestone rocks, surrounded by woodland and skirted by the Kate Brook. The Rocks, together with wool, cider and the little buns called chudleighs, have made the village famous. In the past eager day-trippers travelled from Exeter, either by coach or rail, and today the Rocks still hold a certain, rather ramshackle, appeal for any rambler who relishes scrambling up and down the many twisting paths, and investigating the Kate Brook flowing below.

There is a spectacular waterfall in The Glen, and a famous cavern halfway up the Rocks called the Pixies Hole. This deep cave has two claims to fame − Coleridge wrote about it, and the pixies claim it as their own.

The paths on Chudleigh Rocks provide awkward and sometimes precipitous walking, with dangerous overhangs on the quarry side. No specific directions can be given, but on the assumption that all paths lead to heaven, take the track that climbs, and with any luck you should arrive at the top. Enjoy the splendid view from this open spot before making the return descent.

Climbers and potholers devote much time to the Rocks, and there is a Rock Centre, specialising in caving, abseiling and rock climbing.

After this detour to the Rocks, return to the main road and turn left beside the police house on the corner of Rock Road. Passing the Rock Nursery, it is only a short distance before the next footpath sign appears. This directs us across a field, towards Lawell House in the Clifford Estate. The path crosses the Kate Brook by bridge − look for huge horseshoes nailed to a piece of wood beside the kissing gate. Now follow the wire fence and clear track running beside Lawell House, continuing past enormous oak trees and an avenue of limes, where the footpath emerges into a minor road.

Here the loop walks divide, *the shorter walk* turning right and then right again at the road junction, to return to

Chudleigh by a straight route.

The longer loop, however, turns left into a twisting lane and winds uphill. The tiny hamlet of Gappah − originally Gatepath − lies to the right, but our way turns left, following the ivy-clad wall running beside us.

This old ridge road meanders between a splendid variety of trees, often merging into a green tunnel. On the right, amid its 600 acres and surrounded by lakes and hills, is Ugbrooke House, the home of the Lords Clifford. Originally called Ucga's Brook, it was built by the first Thomas Clifford in the 17th century. The poet Dryden was a constant visitor to this estate and is said to have composed several of his poems here. Behind the wall, the land climbs steeply to the Castle Dyke, a circular camp attributed to the Danes, with outworks of a later date. On the left the woods enclose the quarry below. When the trees end there is a bird's eye view of the village and the surrounding countryside, explaining the siting of this old camp.

Through a green gate on the left, a footpath runs down over a hilly field to Clifford Street, joining the road again just above the cemetery. On the opposite side of Kate Brook, by the bridge, is The Wheel Gift Centre, once Town Mills. Spare time here to browse and recall the past, for the Wheel turns again, and the restored interior shows the old mill in its original working order. Craft workshops and a good restaurant provide interest and relaxation for the tired rambler. The Wheel is open every day from 10 am to 5 pm, except Tuesdays in the winter.

Clifford Street winds narrowly back to the centre of the village. The car park is opposite the junction of the main thoroughfares of the village.

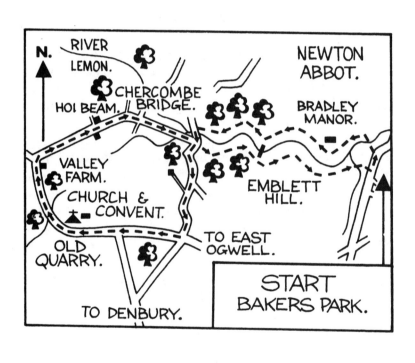

The River Lemon at Newton Abbot

A 3 mile loop walk with an additional 3 mile loop.

A thriving market town, and an excellent centre for reaching many of these walks by bus or train, Newton Abbot has some attractive National Trust countryside fringing its busy hub of roads and shops. This loop walk explores quiet woodland and typical meandering Devon lanes. The walk can be a mere amble along the river Lemon, or a longer walk arising out of the first 3 miles.

A stone's throw from the noisy A381, on the road to Totnes out of Newton Abbot, is Bradley Manor, one of the oldest fortified Tudor houses in Devon. On the western edge of the town and privately occupied, it is open to the public on Wednesday afternoons from April until the end of September.

Cars may be parked at the free, small space inside Baker's Park, where a public footpath on the far side leads through a kissing gate to the banks of the river Lemon. The woodland here is tall and old and peace may be had for the asking – a pleasant thought when relaxing after shopping in town.

Towards the close of the last century, a perfume called Bradley Woods Bouquet was much in demand, sold by a local chemist. Even if the woods don't immediately call this fragrance to mind, the scenery still impresses.

The path runs through Bradley Meadow, beside the mill leat, and alongside the boundary wall of Bradley Manor, reaching a weir with a sluice gate where the water for the leat was originally taken off. A bungalow now occupies the site of old Ogwell Mill, where there is a ford and a footbridge. The way to Chercombe Bridge is interesting, with two steep limestone quarries and adjacent kilns. At the time of walking we observed wintertime forays by flocking goldfinches, while a grey heron flapped away from its customary fishing site, and an extremely acrobatic goldcrest entertained us as we watched it dancing over and under branches in search of food.

The footpath passes through the grounds of Chercombe House, emerging on the bridge. Unfortunately there is no access to the river bank on the opposite side of the Lemon, so to complete the first loop walk it is necessary to retrace your footsteps back to Ogwell Mill and cross the river via the footbridge already mentioned. (See below if you wish to walk the additional loop.)

On this south side of the Lemon the path is sloping and slippery in places. The Puritans' Pit, a huge 20 ft depression with rocky sides, is of great interest; here the first Nonconformists used to meet and worship in the 17th century.

The track divides in the vicinity of the Pit, a higher path providing safer walking than the riverside way. Both paths meet further down river, where an iron bridge spans the water, returning us to Bradley Meadow. Alternatively, it's possible to follow the loops of the river and come into Baker's Park via two stiles and a muddy field.

A further loop may be added on at Chercombe Bridge by walking another 3 miles along quiet country lanes, heading for East and West Ogwell, always turning right and thereby completing a square which returns to Chercombe Bridge. Where the road divides, it is possible to make a ½ mile detour into East Ogwell, where the old part of the village beside the church is attractive. The Jolly Sailor will provide refreshment. Return to West Ogwell Cross and continue on past the convent of the community of The Companions of Jesus the Good Shepherd, once a manor house standing in its own incomparable deerpark. The grounds of the convent are private, but the tiny church of West Ogwell may be visited. It is thought possible that this church, sited on a mound with an oak wood surrounding it, may have a history of early Druid worship. All records are lost, so the imagination may be allowed to wander.

One fact remains, however − the overgrown hollow in the field opposite the church is all that remains of the quarry where pink Ogwell marble came from. Some original stone can be seen in the church.

This is very beautiful pastoral country, with spreading fields balanced by enormous, old trees. These ancient roads twist and bend, weaving their various ways, and charming the walker with the serenity of the beautiful surroundings.

Once back at Chercombe Bridge, retrace your footsteps to Ogwell Mill, as detailed above.

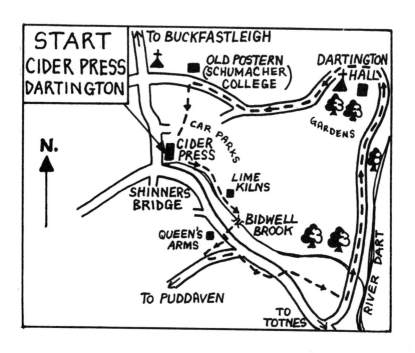

Dartington

A 4 mile loop, with an added stroll around the gardens of Dartington Hall.

Sometimes as much pleasure can be derived from a leisurely stroll in semi-urban surroundings as from an energetic hike over moorland; walking around the gardens and environs of Dartington Hall can give this feeling of reward. A whole day can easily be passed here as there is much to see and enjoy, both in the Cider Press with its craft shops, restaurants and plant centre, and in the gardens of Dartington Hall themselves.

Shinner's Bridge, in the village of Dartington, is some 2 miles beyond Totnes on the A384 road to Buckfastleigh. In 1591, when the bridge was not yet in existence and a ford streamed across the road, this was the home of John Shynner. Here pack ponies loaded with wool and tin passed on their journey from Ashburton to Totnes.

This walk starts at the Dartington Cider Press centre, where there are free car parks. Opening times are from 9.30 am to 5.30 pm from Monday to Saturday all the year round, and Sunday opening in the summer.

Just beyond the Bazaar there is a sign indicating The Riverside Walk, which takes in lime kilns and the Dart Pottery seconds shop. This pleasant, easily negotiated walk follows the Bidwell Brook as it runs parallel to the busy main road. Oak, holly, laurel and the occasional conifer create a charming woodland atmosphere. The two lime kilns have explanatory notices beside them.

After reaching Kingfisher Print & Design Ltd the path forks. Keep to the right-hand track, still following the brook.

Nearly opposite the Queen's Arms, on the other side of the main road, turn right over a footbridge, and cross the (dangerously busy) road. Pick up a path on the opposite side, running parallel to the road, in the direction of Totnes. A 90° turn takes the path to the road leading to Puddaven. Turn left here, returning to the main road. Another path, again leading towards Totnes, brings the path in about 100 yards to a footpath sign on the opposite side of the road. Cross here. This is the right of way that will emerge in the driveway to Dartington Hall.

From here everything settles down into easy walking, away from the traffic of the main road. Wander uphill along this pleasant drive, passing some beautiful views of the river Dart on the right, and on the left horticultural buildings and the Dance Studio, both part of Dartington Hall Trust's educational facilities.

There are two free car parks close to the Hall, but no shop or cafe. Admission to the Gardens is free every day except Bank Holidays, but contributions are invited to assist in the upkeep of this lovely place. It is suggested that organised parties should apply to the Garden Superintendent for permission to visit. All seasons of the year have their own especial attraction here.

An archway leads into the courtyard, built in 1390 by John Holland, Duke of Exeter, and half-brother to Richard II. From the courtyard a path winds towards the Gardens, passing the old kitchen wall and pausing at a lead urn. Take your pick of the many paths that curve away to the various enchantments of the Gardens. Wander at will and, even on a bedraggled winter day, you will find beauty at every turn. Summer foliage may be wonderful, but equally lovely is the silhouette of bough and bare twig against a wild winter sky. Squirrels and birds go about their business uninterrupted. Few tourists invade the Gardens save in the height of the season, and usually only the passing student or absorbed gardener is seen.

Many spectacular views present themselves, every vantage

point having, as it were, a different eye. Don't forget to search out the bronze donkey by Willi Soukop, and Henry Moore's reclining woman, which he described as '. . . a figure of quiet stillness and a sense of permanence as though it could stay there for ever . . .'. Stare upwards at the vast 400 year old chestnuts lining the terrace that overlooks the jousting ground. Appreciate the line of the Twelve Apostles, the row of Irish yews said to have been planted to screen a bear-baiting pit. Within the Gardens are many fine things, but the true climax of the walk must surely be found in the sight of the Hall itself, rising grey-stoned and handsome out of the subtle tones of the tiers of surrounding foliage.

Perhaps the most atmospheric part of Dartington Gardens is the 14th century church tower at the back of the courtyard, all that remains of the original church. This tower is now a chapel, used by the College of Arts, within the Hall. A recent addition is the Japanese garden created close by.

The enormous yew tree shading the old headstones is said to be a thousand years old — could there have been an earlier Saxon church standing here, before the 14th century? Dartington's earliest record dates back to AD 833. In 1878 the church was pulled down, to be rebuilt some 2 miles away, using the old materials, and in the same form. It stands now on the main Ashburton to Totnes road; the return walk passes close to it.

Having explored and enjoyed the Gardens, the walk back to the Cider Press leads away from the Hall, passing through pleasant farming land. Continue down the road, and directly opposite The Old Postern — now the Schumacher College, which specialises in studies of ecological and spiritual values — a cycle track on the left cuts through flat fields. This returns to the entrance to the Cider Press car parks and completes this fascinating walk.

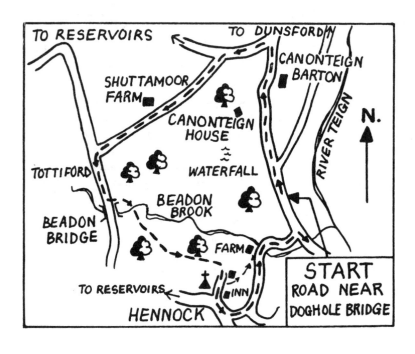

Hennock

A loop walk of 5 miles − hilly walking.

Hennock is a tiny, high-poised village in the Teign valley, reached by winding lanes from Bovey Tracey, turning off the A38(T) from Exeter. There is a bus service from Newton Abbot.

A walk amid this hilly, patchwork-coloured countryside is demanding, but has much to offer by way of reward. A good place to start − parking one's car on a convenient verge of the quiet country road, and avoiding marked 'Passing Places' − is along the road signed Canonteign Waterfall, which turns left at Doghole Bridge, on the west side of the river Teign.

Walking along this road we come to a tall, ivy-draped tower which is a relic of the Adam Williams mine shaft, constructed in 1810. This mine, only one of many in the area, produced copper, manganese, lead and a small amount of silver. Just beyond it stands the ancient Tudor mansion of Canonteign Barton.

This 'house of many gables' as it is described in an old book, was restored from its medieval origin in the first Elizabeth's reign and has experienced the occupation of two armies − King Charles I's Royalist soldiers and more recently American troops in the Second World War. The GIs left peacefully enough, but the Cavaliers defended the old farmhouse against Sir Thomas Fairfax of the Parliamentarian army in 1645 and were defeated.

Originally the house was the seat of the first Viscount Exmouth, but the present Viscount lives in the handsome

Georgian mansion, Canonteign House, standing in its splendid grounds nearby.

Canonteign House Waterfalls and Country Park are open in the summer every day of the week, offering the tourist interesting walks and views of rock formations and streams, set in traditional English countryside. The house is NOT open to the public.

Passing the two houses, the road turns left at North Lodge, signed to Moreton and Bovey. This hill is steep and has wonderful views on a clear day. Continue climbing until a semi-metalled road offers a turn to the left between conifers. This track leads on towards Shuttamoor Farm, remote and old, spread across the road with − keep your eyes open − a grey heron often to be seen fishing in the nearby stream and pond.

In this area the map shows disused mine shafts to the west of the bridge at the bottom of the hill; indeed, the entire district is pitted with relics of mines, and the enthusiast could learn much from a book about the area − *Dartmoor Mines* (see Bibliography).

The hill leads upwards to the reservoirs of Kennick and Tottiford, which feed Torquay. Here one is on top of the world with a view to prove it. When the rhododendrons are in flower around the lanes the beauty is unsurpassable.

Upon reaching a T-junction, turn left and follow the hill that now descends again, passing Tottiford Farm standing in a lovely wild combe with the Beadon Brook jaunting through it. Just before reaching Beadon Bridge, turn left into car parking space at Netton Cleave, which is Forestry Commission property.

Here the public footpath to Hennock turns into the woodland, bearing left. The going can be sticky in bad weather. Cross Beadon Brook by the small wooden footbridge and notice the air valve set beside a stake marked NW. We are now in Great Rock Copse, an area once alive with men and machinery and which closed in 1969 after about 70 years of continuous operation as a lead mine. As mentioned above, fascinating details of the workings of this mine are described in *Dartmoor Mines*. But despite the interest of the area, walkers should be wary of any unauthorised exploration. It is possible to wander along the brook, noticing the possible relics of the mining past — you might even see pieces of the original wooden leat that ran parallel to the water through the woods; it was destroyed in 1978.

The footpath to Hennock, however, does not follow the brook but climbs to the top of the copse. There are some more air valves, and two marker stones bearing the letters TW, M and the year 1858.

At the top of this woodland path, beside some large beech trees, look down and left to see some of the remaining gullies of the mining years.

The footpath ends as it emerges on to a metalled road, with Greatrock Farm on one's right. It continues over the road, beside farm outbuildings, climbing very steeply through trees to a stile and then across a field to a kissing gate in the far right-hand corner. The views here are splendid, with Haldon Belvedere on the left at the end of the ridge of the Haldon Hills, and the villages of Ashton and Chudleigh visible in the valleys below.

Turn left onto a metalled road leading into Hennock, a village which suffered many deaths in times of plague, as did other villages in this remote, hilly area. The church is 15th century with an ancient screen and an even earlier font. The Palk Arms, in the centre of the village, is a freehouse with real ale and good food, an excellent source of refreshment to the weary walker.

Hennock has many attractive old cottages — in particular Longlands House, passed as one enters the village. A medieval hallhouse built in 1450, it was restored in the 17th century. It is now the Longlands Field Centre, running residential educational courses. Visitors are welcome here, and anyone interested in looking over the house has only to ask.

A public footpath runs through Longlands House entrance

yard, providing an *alternative path* back to the starting point of this walk. The path enters a green lane via a gate on the left of Longlands yard, running downhill and emerging in a field. Please shut all gates. Head now for the (hidden) right-hand corner of the field and go through a broken and binder-twine repaired gate into the next field, with brambles dodging every step. Follow the path signed left and downhill, until a footpath sign is found at the bottom left of the field above steps emerging into a lane just above the entrance to Frankland's Farm.

If preferred, however, the walk back to the starting point can be continued through the village, passing the church and the pub and then taking the steep lane signposted 'Teign Village', forking left at Brandiron Cross and reaching the farm that way. 'Brand Iron' is the name given to three-cornered fields and meetings of three roads, and derives from 'brandis iron', a three-legged trivet used in the past to support cooking pots in the hearth.

Both routes back continue on the lane which goes down to Hyner Bridge and then, turning left, reaches Canonteign once more. As a last attraction to a véry beautiful walk, notice the distant waterfall cascading down beneath Birch Cleave Woods, forming an elegant backcloth to Canonteign House, on the left.

Bovey Tracey

Two loop walks of 2½ miles and 2¼ miles.

Bovey Tracey, one of the gateways to Dartmoor, is a small
and pleasant village full of history, lying in rich country at
the foot of Dartmoor. It can be reached by taking the A38
road from Exeter to Plymouth and following the signposts.

These two loop walks are easy, on clearly defined footpaths
and along country roads. Both start and end at the free car
park in the centre of the village beside the bridge and close
to The Old Thatched Inn, a free house.

Leaving the car park, turn left, perhaps on a weekday
pausing to visit the Weaving Shed of the Bovey Handloom
Weavers on the opposite side of Station Road, and then
passing the Dartmoor Hotel on the right. A footpath sign
indicates the way at the corner of Avenue Road, beside
Bowden and Sons Agricultural Engineers. An outlet from
the Pottery leat burbles along beside the road, eventually
running into the river Bovey.

At the T-junction, where Fairfield Close joins Avenue
Road, the way is signed to Chapple, via Challabrook Farm.
A little further on it is necessary to cross a busy main road
− once the line of the old railway − then continue the walk
via a wooden kissing gate on the opposite side of the road.

The footpath again follows the leat, edged now with trees
and grasses. A seat stands beside a cross, with the plaque:
'This old cross once marked the grave of a Royalist Officer
who fell near here, 1645, when Cromwell's troops defeated
the Royalists.' This mutilated medieval cross has had an
interesting history. Originally a waymark, in the days before
signposted roads, it was used, as the plaque says, as a tomb-

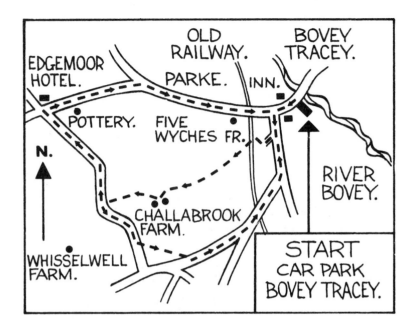

stone for the young officer killed in a Civil War skirmish
on the nearby Heathfield. Some enterprising farmer then took
it for a gatepost, and it was not until 1923 that it was found
and put here, to be admired and revered by locals and visitors
alike.

At the little bridge ahead of us, the leat goes on its separate
way, and we continue through the field gate, following the
straight and often extremely muddy track towards
Challabrook Farm. There is a splendid view of Dartmoor
here, the foothills striding away up to bare heights. The wind
from the moor blows keenly, a slap in the face after leaving
the shelter of the footpath beside the leat. The path goes on,
the view on the right showing impressive woods rising up
to the heights of Hennock village and its neighbouring
countryside.

A wooden gate brings us to the outbuildings of the farm.
At the farm cottages we turn right, the path heading for

Chapple Road, where we leave the farmland and must decide which way to continue the walk − *(A)* or *(B)* below.

(A) If we turn left − a more urban end to the walk − a few yards along the road there is a seat on the bridged trackway of the old Hay Tor Granite Tramway. Beneath flows the Pottery leat, built in 1850 to bring water down to Bovey Tracey Potteries. Laid in 1820, the clumsy stone trackways of the Tramway carried horse-drawn trucks for 8 miles, bearing granite hewn from Hay Tor quarries down to the canal at Teigngrace. Here barges were loaded and poled down to Teignmouth and the stones then taken by sea to London, where they were used to build part of London Bridge as well as many other public buildings.

Some 150 yards down the road, we take the Public Bridleway signposted to the left. This is the Templer Way, a walk suitable for wheelchairs, as the disabled motif indicates. Along this rather muddy lane are constant reminders of the Granite Tramway. At the end of the lane we turn left into Moor View, continuing on to pass the post office, go over the bridge, and follow the road to return to the car park, the starting point of the walk.

It is possible at the entry into Moor Lane to continue straight on, along another 100 yards or so of the Bridleway, and then turn left; this forms an extra loop which passes the old Pottery Pond, used for many years to power Bovey Tracey Potteries. A footpath edges the pond, returning to a point just below the post office, mentioned above.

(B) Or we can turn right for a journey, by road, back to the car park in the middle of the village.

Sections of the Granite Tramway appear all along the verge of this road, on the left-hand side, and the track is very plain before it disappears into Chapple Wood, where one of the original milestones is said to be still in place.

Chapple Road takes us through a canopy of beautiful trees, uphill past a bridlepath sign to Brimley via Whisselwell Farm, and continues on to a four crossway. The hill to the left goes to Hay Tor, this being the entrance to the Dartmoor National

Park, but we turn right, passing the Edgemoor Hotel on our left as we go downhill. This old house with its gracious grounds was once Bovey Tracey Grammar School.

Some 60 yards on the right is Lowerdown Pottery, run by David Leach, and open to visitors Monday to Friday from 9 am to 1 pm and 2 pm to 6 pm, with visiting on Saturdays by appointment only. Continue down the hill — paying careful attention to traffic and passing picturesque Five Wyches Farm and its old stone barn, both thatched, in the original style of farm buildings.

This road continues to a junction where an old milestone stands. Here turn right, following down into Bovey Tracey, passing the Dartmoor Gateway Restaurant, and, opposite the roundabout on the left, noticing the remains of Bovey's old railway station, first used in 1866 and now used for industrial purposes.

The Dartmoor Hotel is on our right and at the point where the A382 to Exeter or to Newton Abbot is signed we pass the Dolphin Hotel, which ran a coaching service in 1882, with four trips weekly over surrounding moorland.

Cross the road, passing Brookside Tea Rooms, to return to the car park.

Moretonhampstead

A walk of 3½ miles with a possible loop of an extra ½ mile.

Moretonhampstead, on the A382 road from Bovey Tracey, or turning off the A30(T) at Whiddon Down, was once an important market town before roads and railways linked the moorland villages. Today its importance has faded, but an immense charm prevails. It lies in a bowl of fertile land on the fringe of eastern Dartmoor and is a splendid place for touring and, in particular, for walking. There are several good pubs and various tea shops in the village.

This walk is a quiet amble over footpaths, twisting Devon lanes and a small chunk of open moorland with near-panoramic views. Where the Bovey Tracey road enters the village there is a large free car park, and from here it is only a step to the centre of the village.

A visit to the church is recommended, with perhaps a glance at the graves of French officers who died on parole during the Napoleonic wars. The handsome almshouses, built in 1637, are still inhabited, and close by the churchyard is Cross Cottage, a memory of the famous Dancing Tree where a platform was raised among immense branches to provide footing for a fiddler who played to the dancing villagers below.

Take the road signed Mardon and Clifford, going downhill across a brook and looking out for the footpath on the right as the hill begins to climb. The footpath is signed Yarningdale and Mardon (Shute Lane) and stands at the entrance to Halscombe Farm. To the right, and below the hillside, stands Mardon House, with its attractive garden.

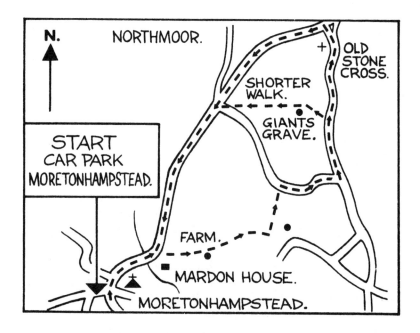

Follow the track and at Halscombe Farm take the signed path to Mardon, crossing a wooden stile and entering what appears to be a green tunnel. This is typical of Devon's sunken lanes, sometimes known as hollow lanes and very often in the past providing hidden ways for smugglers. These lanes, being sheltered, are often starred with early flowers. Snowdrops, primroses, bluebells and foxgloves can be seen here during the varying seasons. Mud is the prime decoration in winter and it is, perhaps, humbling to consider what our ancestors endured when travelling the countryside.

We go ever upwards, wondering if the hill is one in three as it seems so steep — but there are occasional places where a peep through the hedge offers tantalising views which make the ascent very worthwhile.

Shute Lane contains evidence of vigorous badger activity, with lots of snout-marks disturbing the banks. Through an iron kissing gate and on, passing a footpath signing the way back to the village, the lane now becomes semi-metalled,

36

passing the bungalow called Heathercrest. Fifty yards further on turn left through a newish wooden gate and then keep heading for Mardon. There is plenty to look at, with the village a grey cluster below the hill, and occasional old granite gate posts along the way. The view becomes quite magnificent, with a semi-circle of Dartmoor laid out for inspection. This is wonderful countryside, with birds and insects abounding and only occasional farming noises to break the serene solitude.

At the top of this lane there is a wooden stile and a gate. Here a cart track leads to the road, where we turn right and then left at the next junction. The road is signed Smallridge and approximately ¼ mile further on, where two windswept trees mark the spot, it is possible to turn left, climbing the moorland in search of the Giant's Grave. The Grave is actually all that remains of a cairn, originally a Bronze Age grave which was topped with turf and then stones. This track continues due west, eventually meeting the junction of two roads, down which the return loop of the walk descends to the village.

If, however, you decide to omit the Giant's Grave from your walk, continue along the road to Smallridge until tracks on the right merge with the road at a stone called the Headless Cross. This is an example of a medieval waymark, now sadly mutilated by time and erosion. Turn left at the next road junction, and eventually arrive at the place where the track from the Giant's Grave emerges.

As said before, the views from the top of the moorland path are near-panoramic, taking in Dartmoor to the south and west and the distant smudge of Exmoor to the north, far beyond the steep wooded sides of the Teign gorge. The huge rocky prominence visible to the south east is Blackingstone Rock, over 1,000 feet above sea level and said to be the haunt of King Arthur and the Devil long ago, when the quoits these two characters played with fell as granite outcrop.

At the junction of the moorland path with the two merging

roads, cross the cattle-grid and return to Moretonhampstead, via a splendidly twisting road.

Lustleigh

A 6 mile loop walk, with an alternative 3½ mile loop.

The village of Lustleigh, ½ mile off the Bovey Tracey to Moretonhampstead A382 road, is a most attractive walking area, combining fields, country lanes and open moorland. It can be reached by bus from Newton Abbot.

The starting point of these two loop walks is Hammerslake, to the north west of Lustleigh, and arrived at via Rudge and Pethybridge. Cars may be parked in a small layby in this quiet country road, where a footpath is signed into surrounding woodland. Take the path marked Hunter's Tor, up through trees, bearing right and emerging on the top of a ridge with impressive moorland views. One of the joys of this walk is the variety of both terrain and scenic views, coupled with the fact that one is never out of earshot of the river Bovey, far below. After the somewhat tricky path through the trees, with enormous rocky outcrops and hazardous roots, it is good to feel flat turf beneath the feet, following the ridge path towards Hunter's Tor. Here bluebells run riot in late spring, together with foxgloves and a panoply of small green plants, together with gorse, bracken and wild broom.

Take time to look at your map, matching up the landmarks all around. Hay Tor looms into view as the path progresses, Manaton church leads the eye further eastward to the stone finger of Bowerman's Nose, with Hameldon in the distance and the immense shoulder of Cosdon in the north, haze or mist permitting. Behind you, the country landscape ends with the long ridge of Haldon, sloping down to Teignmouth's 'bite', with the sea beyond.

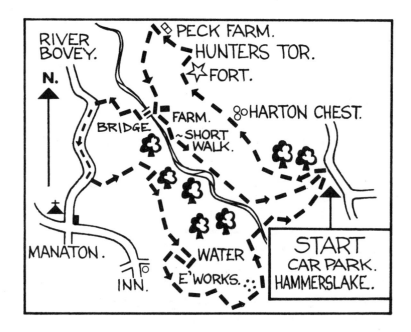

The ancient Bronze Age camp of Hunter's Tor, with its still visible circular ramparts, stands on the highest point of the ridge, and from here the way goes downhill, leaving moorland and entering farmland, with its perennial hazard of muddy paths. In winter the mud really is deep — be warned.

A signposted gate — 'Path' — takes us down the hillside towards Peck Farm, through a field beside the farmhouse and left, after the fieldgate, into a lane. After passing a pond on the left, follow the signposted path to Foxworthy Bridge. This attractive farm path, though wet and difficult in winter is delightful in spring, with wild flowers in plenty and fields on the right-hand side stretching down to the river. Along these farm lanes, in centuries past, packhorses and donkeys travelled, loaded high with all sorts of merchandise and farm crops. Then they were routes of commerce, now they have become pleasant walking paths for people at leisure. Times change!

Another sign of change can be seen passing the wonderful old house of Foxworthy Farm, now renovated, with modernised barns alongside it. Foxworthy Bridge spans the river Bovey, and here the walks split up, the shorter one following the footpath sign to Hammerslake via Foxworthy Mill. (For the longer walk see *(B)* below.)

(A) This shorter way takes a woody path after the gate just past the old mill, returning us to the Cleave, but this time along the floor of it, no longer in the heights. The woodland is varied, but mostly oak, holly, hazel and birch, with lots of wildflowers at all seasons. In particular, the Cleave is renowned for its bluebells.

The many footpaths traversing the Cleave are very well signposted these days, and no longer does one stumble along through bracken and scrub, wondering which track leads to where. There is a folk legend that a party of Tudor horsemen haunt the Cleave; maybe they are still trying to find their way to Lustleigh.

The path begins to climb very slowly, but don't be fooled – before you reach the ridge path above you will be puffing! Lichens decorate the rocky outcrops, and stone crop, moss, whortleberries, ferns and many other lovely things help the walker along. Do pause and look down at the palette of colours spread out below. In spring the warm purple of budding hazel is a joy.

The path eventually joins the ridge above, turning right, and then retracing its way back to Hammerslake.

(B) The longer loop walk leaves Foxworthy behind, crossing the bridge beyond the farm and then taking the signed footpath up to the country road leading left into Manaton. Here the village green affords rest after the steep climb. The church invites a visit – notice the painted panels said to have been mutilated by Cromwell's men in the Civil War.

To return, head back down the hill for a very short distance and opposite the village hall, turn into Slinker's Lane. This path is very wet in bad weather, but provides good walking and is a wonderful example of the old medieval bridleways with which Devon is blessed.

At the T-junction turn right to the old-world hamlet of Water. If required a detour may be made here to the Kes Tor Inn, not far down the Bovey Tracey road, where the bar snacks and ale are good. Otherwise continue past the little 'green' of Water, turning left into the old Manaton Road, walking south east, passing Beckhams Farm, and finally descending a tunnel-like rough track which is the original main road from Bovey Tracey to Manaton, used regularly before the present road was cut into the hillside in the middle of the 19th century.

At the bottom of this road it is possible to turn right and climb up to Becky Falls, where a popular café is sited (open in the summer season) just above the tumbling waters of the Becka Brook.

Otherwise turn left at the bottom of the old Manaton Road and climb the path bordering on Houndtor Wood, passing an old earthwork and enjoying the lush vegetation all around. Here in spring, when rain has fallen and the feeder streams which run down the hillside are full, primroses abound. Wood sorrel grows over moss on fallen branches, and birds sing their territorial rights with abandon. Later, in May, bluebells cast a colourful haze everywhere, and particularly in Lustleigh Cleave, to which this path eventually descends, arriving at Clam Bridge.

The bridge is made of split tree trunks, with a hand rail on one side, and marks a crossing of the river Bovey where in the past packhorse trains forded the waters.

After crossing the bridge, a decision must be made: to follow the footpath signed Hammerslake is to opt for the easier walk − turning left and following the riverside is more challenging, and in winter should not be attempted, as some of the path is flooded by the turbulent river. If this path is followed, the walk will be extended by another 1½ miles but for dedicated ramblers it could well prove a bonus.

The small winding path is hazardous with huge boulders and trailing roots. It is necessary from time to time to make little deviations in order to avoid impassable inlets. But, keeping always within sight of the river, and pausing half-way along to enjoy the tremendous force of the water as it syphons through holes between vast, moss-covered boulders, eventually we arrive close to Foxworthy Mill, where a footpath signs us back to Hammerslake.

If the easier path is taken, after crossing Clam Bridge, then the starting point of Hammerslake, on the ridge, is reached sooner but without the exhilarating thrill of having faced the many challenges of the river path.

Back in Lustleigh, The Cleave Hotel and Primrose Cottage Tea Rooms offer refreshment to the weary walker.

Manaton to Easdon Down

A 4 mile walk.

Manaton is a typical, rather remote, fringe-of-the-moor village approximately 5 miles south of Moretonhampstead and the same distance north of Bovey Tracey. It has a lovely 15th century church and warmly thatched old granite houses ringing the capacious green. As a starting point for many walks it is ideal, catering for the intrepid moor walker as well as those who prefer the easy leisure of lanes and footpaths. It can be reached by the B3344 road from Bovey Tracey, and the B3212 from Moretonhampstead, which joins the B3344 at Beetor Cross, known locally as 'The Watching Place'.

This walk is a short, easy ramble of some 4 miles, which encompasses moorland, country lane and footpath. Cars may be left in the free park beside the church. The Kes Tor Inn, ½ mile down the road towards Bovey Tracey, has excellent bar snacks. Further down the road still and picturesquely placed in the trees, is the Becky Falls Café, again with its own car park.

Starting from the footpath sign outside Manaton church, we cross the churchyard. Just beyond the mutilated medieval cross (a signpost from the past) the footpath turns right, leading us to nearby Manaton Rocks where, in spring, the bluebells are thick and beautiful.

It is believed that these rocks were the site of a Royalist battery in the Civil War of 1642-48; imagination boggles at the thought of the strength needed to haul a cannon up these heights.

From the top of the rocks the view is almost panoramic

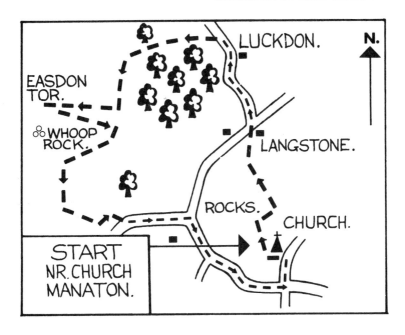

on a clear day, with our next port of call, Easdon Tor, rising to the north west. Following the arc south, we can see Hameldown in the far distance to the east, with the strange rock formation known as Bowerman's Nose rising up from Hayne Down in the near foreground. Who was Bowerman? Some say he actually lived in William the Conqueror's day – others that the name is a derivation of the Celtic words for 'great stone'. Take your pick.

From Manaton Rocks we follow the path bearing right, and join with another path leading north west through pleasant country scenery, following yellow waymarks on stile and trees. This brings us out on to the country road close to Langstone Farm. Turn right here, continuing along the lane to Lower Luckdon. Just beyond Lower Luckdon there is a gate with a 'North Haye' sign and a footpath directing us to Barracot via Easdon. Follow the orange waymarks to Easdon Hill. This path climbs steeply through a plantation and is hard going, finally emerging on to rough moorland.

When leaving the woodland, Easdon Tor is ahead of you on the hill above, with many tracks leading to it through heather and bracken. Make a small diversion here by climbing to the Tor, to look at the countryside around and below. Just beneath the Tor a rock formation called Whooping Rock is supposed, in the past, to have held miraculous powers for curing children with whooping cough. There are Bronze Age hut circles and cairns, as well as boundary stones, spread out on this slope of Easdon Down, which can provide interesting archaeological discoveries.

Leaving the Tor and returning to the path, we follow the bridlepath to the apex of conifer plantation, and then continue on until we reach the corner of a stone wall. Follow the wall, turning left quite shortly, and descend to the county road by way of a farm track, entered left via a gate where a Public Bridleway signs the way we have come from Lower Luckdon Farm. This track merges with the road below.

At Langstone Cross road junction take the Manaton road, returning to the village through pleasant farmlands. A short cut is signed first on the right-hand side of the road, and then, nearing the church, on the left. This is the ancient Church Path.

A short walk, but quiet, and full of beauty and interest.

Hay Tor to Hound Tor

A loop walk of 7 miles and a shorter diversion of some 2½ miles.

This moorland walk begins at Upper Terrace Drive, near Hay Tor Rocks. Take the Hay Tor road out of Bovey Tracey and follow it uphill until a minor road turns right opposite a disused petrol station, just before the turn left to Ilsington, where a telephone kiosk stands on a triangle of grass. Behind it is the Moorland Hotel.

This minor road is Upper Terrace Drive. A short distance along the road, on the left, stands a stone marker which is the start of these two walks. Cars may be parked on the moorland verge further up the hill. The long walk includes some rough walking, following ups and downs, and possibly some marshy ground. The return loop is by moorland road, but this can be eased by using the verges. The short diversion along the Hay Tor Granite Tramway is all moorland.

The usual warning must be given about not walking on Dartmoor in the mist, and always having map and compass to safeguard oneself, for weather conditions can change very fast. It is *not safe* to wander in the vicinity of quarries and rubble heaps in less than perfect conditions.

If you intend to follow the Tramway and visit the quarries, you will find a little reading beforehand will enhance your pleasure. Derek Beavis's book, in particular − *The Templer Way* − gives very full descriptions of what to look for, together with details of quarry working and social conditions of the past. Briefly, the Granite Tramway was laid in 1820 to carry granite from the quarries to Teignmouth, which also included transportation by barge down the Stover Canal.

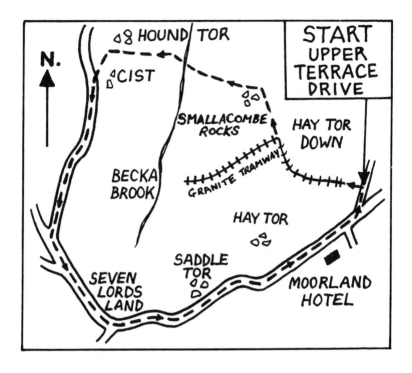

The Tramway, made of the very stone being mined, was powered by horse-drawn wagons which descended the 1,300 ft incline to the canal, from whence it was barged to Teignmouth. When London Bridge was rebuilt, Dartmoor granite was used.

In the spring and summer, the Dartmoor National Park Authority organises guided walks in this fascinating area; these are both informative and entertaining. The free *Dartmoor Visitor* includes a schedule of such walks.

Both these walks begin by following the Tramway as it climbs Hay Tor Down — using the stone marker as the starting point. *(A)* About 1 mile from the start, a wide track leaves the Tramway turning right towards nearby Smallacombe Rocks. This is the way to Hound Tor and the route of the *longer loop walk.* For the shorter walk see *(B)* below.

Near the rocks there is a group of hut circles, ruins of what was a very early farm. Pottery excavated here dates the occupation from 1300 BC. As a romantic walker, I find it easy to imagine much activity among these stones — children playing, and women cooking over their fires, awaiting the return of their menfolk from tending stock and crops. And as I climb down the hillside towards the Becka Brook below, I wonder at the hard work entailed in carrying water up — every day.

There are several paths leading down to the brook. Just before you reach it you will pass a blue waymarked bridlepath sign to Leighton (right) and one onwards to Houndtor Down. A clapper bridge crosses the brook and then the steep, rocky path climbs upwards towards a gate and another bridlepath sign. From here the path is plain. Make a short detour to Greator Rocks, on the left, and look through a cleft in the stony wall, for the view of the valley below is beautiful. In the autumn rowan berries, gorse and fading, foxy bracken weave a colourful tapestry. And there is an aspect of Hay Tor not usually seen, with Black Hill and Hay Tor Down behind us and Trendlebere Down in the distance.

As at Smallacombe Rocks, this hillside in the past must have been very busy. Our path passes through the remains of a medieval settlement, as we climb towards Hound Tor. There are eleven ruined dwellings in all, excavated in the 1960s to reveal remains dating back to the 13th and 14th centuries, with evidence of an earlier settlement, perhaps of the 8th century, before that. The village was deserted — perhaps when the Black Death struck, or for reasons that still remain a mystery.

Hound Tor, looming above, is perhaps the most spectacular pile of rock on the moor; it looks primeval and unwelcoming, and many are the folktales centred around it. In particular, it is said to be a haunt of that well known inhabitant of Dartmoor, the Devil.

From the top of the Tor, yet another view shows itself — Hameldown lies like a stranded whale to the west, with the chunky piles of Honeybag Tor in the foreground. Aim at re-joining the road south west of the Tor, and search for a ruined cist, or burial place, in the heather.

And this is not the only burial place in the area — ¾ mile along the road, to the east, lies the grave of poor Kitty Jay, hanged in a nearby barn and for ever after banished to a lonely plot of ground in the middle of a moorland track, at the point of three parish boundaries. One of the typical Dartmoor tales insists that it is the pixies who keep her grave decorated with fresh flowers. Pixie or human, the flowers are always there.

The road, turning left from Hound Tor, winds along in a half-circle, back to the starting place. It is possible to cut corners here and there, but the ground is often marshy. Look out for the castle-like profile of Bonehill Rocks and for the square outlines of ancient cultivations at Foales Arrishes, under the hillside of Pil Tor, where the roads meet at Hemsworthy Gate.

Seven Lords Land, where seven boundaries meet, lies to the left as the road sweeps onwards to Hay Tor. On the right Rippon Tor flies red flags when firing is in operation in the summer. Between Saddle Tor and Hay Tor there are boundary stones and watch for the many varied faces that the rocks present — a sphinx, an Indian, the choice is yours.

The last view of this walk is different from what we have become used to, but equally magnificent. Against the horizon the Haldon Belvedere stands out impressively and the coastline spreads itself to well beyond Berry Head, the Channel clear, even on a grey day.

In the car park beneath Hay Tor Rocks there is usually an ice cream van, and the Moorland Hotel is close by. Follow the road back to Upper Terrace Drive, our starting place.

(B) For the shorter diversion-walk, continue following the Granite Tramway along its entire length, taking time to divert along the first branch line, on the left, which leads to Hay Tor Quarry. The entrance is by climbing an incline to an unlocked gate. After exploring this small, sheltered world, which has now become a rich habitat for both flora and fauna,

and perhaps gaining some idea of the intense work that the granite industry demanded in the 19th century, return to the main line, following it as it leads further across the moorland.

The tracks approaching Holwell Quarry are not as clear as the earlier line, but discovering cuttings, points and slag heaps of discarded granite, and realising that this was once an industrial site, will certainly offset any difficulties that may present themselves in following the line.

When enough has been absorbed, just turn back and follow the line downhill, back to the stone marker at Upper Terrace Drive, sparing a thought as you do so for the wild life that now has the whole overgrown site as a hunting and breeding ground. Times change, indeed.

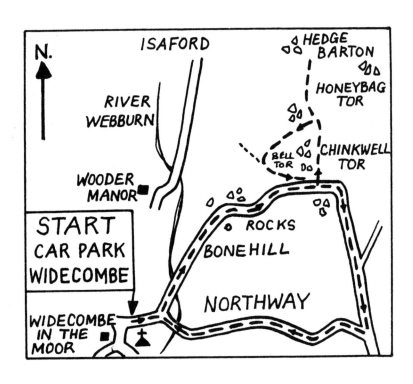

Widecombe In The Moor

A loop walk of 3 miles with an alternative loop of 1¾ miles.

Widecombe in the Moor can be reached by car via the A384 road from Two Bridges to Ashburton, or the B3212 from Two Bridges to Moretonhampstead.

Most visitors to Dartmoor know and love Widecombe, with its handsome church, surrounding village green and attendant cluster of cafés and gift shops. But even Uncle Tom Cobley palls at times, and the walk up Bonehill and on to Honeybag Tor does much to clear the mind of grey mares and pixies, enabling the walker to see Widecombe in its proper perspective − as a jewel of a moorland village with a long, fascinating history, set amid the richness and ever-changing colours of the enclosing countryside.

This walk covers approximately 3 miles − but remember to add extra for all the hills you climb. The way is mostly by road, which means you can walk on the moorland verge, and there is much to see as you walk. The alternative loop to Honeybag Tor is a moorland path. Be warned − these hills are breathtaking!

Passing out of Widecombe with the church on our right − and do visit the church; it has an amazing story to tell − we turn left on leaving the village. This is Bonehill, winding up out of the valley, bridging the burbling East Webburn river and fascinating visitors with its embellishment of enormous grey boulders and ancient farmsteads. There seems to be no record of why it is called Bonehill, nor of the derivation of the name Honeybag. These are mysteries that Dartmoor delights in, leaving much scope for the imagination of the walker.

The farms dotted on each side of Bonehill were all in existence by the 16th century and at least one of them is a typical example of the original 'longhouse', when stock and humans lived under one roof. Even today on Bonehill, with some restoration work in evidence, the atmosphere of age remains undimmed.

At the top of the hill, Bonehill Rocks loom large and spectacular on our right. *The detour to Honeybag Tor* takes us left here, up the track leading to the first tor nearby. Its rock basins were originally thought to be of Druid origin but are now known to be merely the result of erosion. So much for legend. This is Bell Tor, and from here the track continues to Chinkwell Tor, crowned with cairns. (If you are not taking the detour, continue at *(A)* below.)

Cairns are generally connected with ancient burial grounds and so we automatically look for hut circles which, sure enough, are scattered on the western side of the slope below the tor. Bronze Age man lived here in an era of warmer weather, burying his dead on high ground nearby.

Above the circles is Slades Well, marked by a boundary stone. Here a spring forms a muddy pool where sheep and ponies drink. At the time of walking a pair of ravens emerged from their roost ahead of us, somewhere among the rocks of Honeybag Tor.

From the top of Honeybag there is an almost panoramic view. To the west is the valley of Widecombe, with the village a mere cluster of houses crowding around the church. Behind us is Hound Tor, with its ferocious facade of teeth-like rock. Northwards the ground slopes down to Hedge Barton, and on our left rises the huge, whale-shaped ridge of Hameldown, marked by occasional bumps of barrows or burial grounds where Bronze Age chieftains were laid to rest. Moormen used to say that from the top of Hameldown the whole of Devon could be seen − on a fine day. It's worth climbing to find out if the saying is true.

If you prefer to return to Bonehill Rocks by the same route this is easy enough, and of course the views change as you retrace your steps. But another way, of roughly the same distance, takes us down a track, mid-way between Chinkwell and Honeybag Tors, towards woodland at the bottom of the slope. Here a rough road turns left, following the contours of the land, returning us to the top of Bonehill. As you walk, look left at the rocks above and notice the effects of erosion on the granite — with a little imagination faces and shapes appear. There are several rocks which seem to be balancing precariously on the apex of others, but true logan, or logging rocks, are rare to find.

(A) Arriving back at Bonehill, continue walking along the road leading south west over Bonehill Down, turning sharp left at the next junction and returning to Widecombe by the more usual approach down North Hill. The road is busy in the ·season and so it is advisable to walk upon the verge. Pleasant excursions may, of course, be made into the moorland running alongside this steep hill. Top Tor and Hollow Tor, on the left, are easily reached and afford good resting places with excellent viewpoints.

Widecombe, at the bottom of the hill, has at least two tea houses and also two pubs — The Old Inn, where excellent bar snacks may be had, and The Rugglestone Inn just outside the village on the Venton road, a lovely little inn still keeping to its old way of life, but offering no bar food.

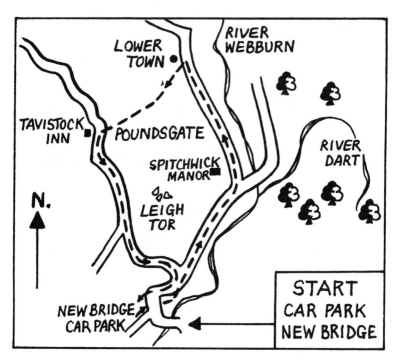

First loop walk from New Bridge to Poundsgate.

New Bridge

A 4 mile loop walk, and a 3 mile loop walk, with an additional loop of 4 miles extra.

New Bridge, one of the 'honey-pot' areas of Dartmoor, spans the river Dart as it loops and wanders through the woodland bordering the fringe of the moor. It stands on the Ashburton to Dartmeet road (reached by the A38(T) from Exeter to Plymouth), a handsome grey stone bridge with three arches and pointed buttresses.

Beside it is a large free car park, with toilets and a Dartmoor National Park Authority Information Centre. Often ice cream vans, with perhaps tea or coffee also, call here. Two pleasant, shortish walks start from this point, going in opposite directions, using footpaths and quiet lanes, with only a short area of busy road to negotiate on the return loops. New Bridge is an ideal spot for a family day out in summer, with the river, sandy little coves, and easy paths through the glorious woodland, as well as the Information Centre to answer all queries about the countryside, with maps, books, postcards etc on sale.

The first walk is a loop of approximately 4 miles which starts in the car park, passing beneath the bridge, and then follows the bank of the river. The lovely woodlands of Holne Chase are on the right-hand side of the Dart, and the rugged face of Leigh Tor on the left. Dominating the skyline is the eminence of Buckland Beacon, which is over 1,200 ft. On the stones at the summit of this tor are inscribed the Ten Commandments, and the view from that point is quite unforgettable.

When the path along the river joins the Buckland-in-the-

Moor road, turn right for a short distance, passing Spitchwick Lower Lodge, then left at the fork signed Lower Town, and look for a footpath to Poundsgate on the left as you climb the steep hill. The footpath sign stands beside a postbox close to a farmhouse. The path passes old Monkswell Cottage, with its hanging slate-clad walls, and goes through a gate marked by a yellow waymark. Follow the high holly hedge and look left at the splendid view. We are in open country now, with sloping fields and neatly trimmed hedges making a nice contrast to the distant moorland vistas. Continue on through several gates until eventually the path turns left into a narrow road, which is merely marked 'Path'. Ignore the next footpath, signed to Townwood Cottages, and turn right, passing the imposing entrance to Spitchwick Manor, one of the five ancient manors of Widecombe parish, eventually emerging into the road in Poundsgate just before the Tavistock Inn (left) is reached. The traffic along this road is dangerous and care must be taken, particularly in the summer season.

The Tavistock Inn is reputed to have once entertained the Devil in the form of a horseman. It is said he stirred his beer with a fire and brimstone hoof before continuing on his way to Widecombe, where he wreaked havoc on the church.

The road winds steeply back towards New Bridge, through open moorland, and it is wise to walk well away from the road verge. Perhaps a bit of scrambling around the clitter of Leigh Tor would be enjoyable before reaching the bridge.

The second loop walk starts by crossing New Bridge to a small car park beside a wooden stile, where there is a footpath through the National Trust woodland. Before climbing the stile, do look at the two large granite posts which support it − they are moorstone gateposts, used for centuries and now again in constant use.

The footpath is an easy, wide track, passing beneath

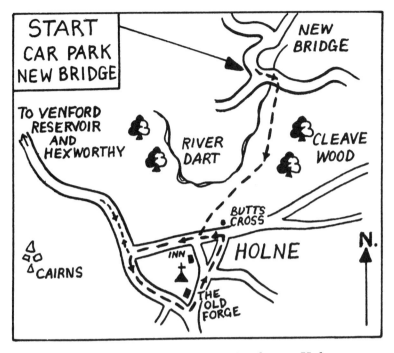

Second loop walk from New Bridge to Holne.

huge deciduous trees, with a lot of holly dotted around —
Holne being a derivation of that common plant's name. In
spring primroses abound, and there are also some drifts of
snow-drops. But the daffodils which seem to grow
everywhere are not the small wild flowers which sometimes
are indigenous to river banks; these are descended from
commercial plantings of the past, grown in a field close to
the footpath at Lower Town in the above walk, which since
then have spread widely over the locality.

When the river runs high, in winter or even early spring,
the noise of the rushing white water is like thunder. Patterns
are made by the force of the river as it rushes over the rocks
and boulders in its path. In summer, the quiet trickle is
tamer — and much safer.

The footpath, signed to Holne, leads left and upwards,

59

although a pleasant, additional walk can be taken by following the river and exploring the bank-side paths before returning to the footpath sign.

With Cleave Woods left behind, the path emerges in a meadow and continues through several stiles, finally joining the road which turns right towards Hexworthy. Where this road joins the lower road from Holne (left), walkers with energy to spare may like to add another *four mile loop,* walking through open moorland to lovely Venford Reservoir. Above the reservoir Bench Tor can easily be climbed. High and awesome, it hangs over the gorge of the Dart, with views which reward one for the extra mileage walked.

The lower road to Holne, on the return trip, takes us into the village. The Old Forge, in season, offers delectable refreshment, also the old Church House Inn. In the churchyard notice the engaging tombstone with an epitaph that has made Poor Old Ned quite famous.

The road returns north through the village, turning left at Butts Cross for approximately 50 yards, and then taking the signed footpath back through Cleave Woods to New Bridge, below.

Dartmeet

A loop walk of 3 miles, with an optional loop of another 3 miles.

Perhaps the most famous beauty spot on Dartmoor, Dartmeet lies at the confluence of the waters of the East and West Dart rivers. On the A384 road from Ashburton to Two Bridges, it has a large free car park with toilets and facilities for buying tea and soft drinks in the summer season. Badger's Holt Cafe, at the further end of the car park, provides lunches and cream teas and has a gift shop. It is open seasonally.

Dartmeet, with its historic clapper bridge and tumbling waters lapping smooth grey boulders, is very beautiful; but more beauty awaits the dedicated walker, just out of sight.

On this walk, the way lies parallel with the river, starting at the footpath signed Cator Gate via Sherwell, near the entrance to Badger's Holt Cafe. Soon this clear track climbs north east, hugging the side of Yar Tor and finally arriving at the road to Sherwell and Babeny from Oldsbrim, by way of the Sherwell enclosures.

Be warned − too much adventurous foraging away from the footpath results in ploughing through boggy land and shoulder-high bracken which, although exhilarating, can also be frustrating and very time-consuming.

The path emerges on the road by way of a stile. Having turned right, a decision must now be made − either *(B)* to continue on the second loop by taking the footpath signed to Cator Gate, some 200 yards down the road, or to head back to Dartmeet *(A)*, thereby finishing the first 3 mile loop.

(A) If the latter is decided upon, then follow the road winding along between Corndon Tor, left, and Yar Tor,

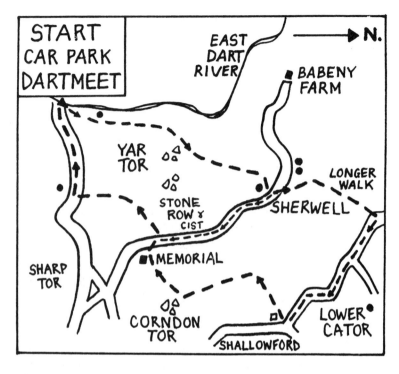

right, until a clear track climbs to Yar Tor. Before leaving the road, perhaps make a short diversion to look at the memorial on the left, raised to Lt E.A. Cave-Penny, who died in Palestine in 1918, aged 19.

The path heading for Yar Tor passes quite close to another burial place, between 2,000 and 3,000 years old — a Bronze Age cist called the Moneypit. Not far from the road, this cist is set within a retaining circle of stones and lies near the remnants of a triple stone row. Many of these stones were vandalized by road and wall-builders during the last century, and the rows are not easy to find now. They lead north-westward to a barrow, and can provide a fascinating exercise in detection.

The lower slopes of Yar Tor hold evidence of other primitive habitation; there is one particularly large hut circle, and on the opposite side of the hill running down to

Dartmeet, another ruined hut circle on the track leading to Rowbrook Farm.

Other, more modern farmers also worked this ground, and it is said that potatoes were grown here during the Napoleonic wars. There may be furrows and lynchets beneath the bracken but these, like the old stones, take some finding.

From Yar Tor you can either pick your way through moorland back to the car park, or play safe and follow the main road down. There are many more hut circles and enclosure remains dotted all around this old road. The famous coffin stone hides itself on the opposite side — a memory of days gone by when funeral processions rested their heavy loads on the long, low slab of rock, and small crosses and initials were cut into the stone by the bearers as they rested briefly.

Back at Dartmeet, be sure to inspect the old clapper bridge and listen to the river singing. The old saying has a certain chill about it — 'River of Dart, River of Dart, Every year thou claimest a heart.'

(B) The second loop walk begins in Sherwell, taking the signed footpath to Cator Gate. Turning left off the road, it is an easy track to follow. It crosses open moorland, shortly joining the country road where the sign to 'Grey Goose' proclaims Cator Gate, close by. Turn right here and continue along the road for approximately 1 mile, to the entrance to Shallowford Farm. Opposite the entrance road, on the right-hand side of the road we are walking, is a cement platform for milk churns, and this marks the start of the return path over Corndon.

Avoid the boggy ground at the start of this path. Straight ahead of you, and upward, are two thorn trees silhouetted against the ridge. Take this as a pointer and climb towards them. On the ridge, turn left and pass between the two cairns on Corndown Tor. The views are very fine all around and one can play the familiar game of naming the many landmarks. In particular Sharp Tor, with its unmistakable shape, is eye-catching.

From the cairns, search out the memorial of Lt Cave-Penny below, and walk towards it. From here, follow the return route to Dartmeet, as detailed above on the shorter walk.

Two Bridges

A loop walk of 3¼ miles, or alternative loop of 4½ miles.

Two Bridges is not even a village. Situated at the junction of two roads traversing Dartmoor — the A384 and the B3212 — it consists of (naturally) two bridges, an hotel and a cottage.

For this walk, and for walk 15, it is important to be aware of activity on the three firing ranges on Dartmoor. Walkers are advised to seek day to day information before they plan their walks, from police stations, information centres and post offices, or by ringing direct to The Range Liaison Officer, DEVCOR Training Areas, Seaton Barracks, Tavistock Road, Plymouth, Tel: Plymouth 772312, extension 249.

At all times, watch for red lights and flags warning of Ministry of Defence artillery and rifle practice. There is no firing in August, but it continues throughout the remainder of the year including some weekends.

The walk begins at the point between the cottage and the quarry opposite the hotel, where it is possible to park cars. A footpath sign directs the way to Wistman's Wood, and at lambing time there is always a notice instructing walkers to keep dogs on the lead. Follow the very eroded path to the next stile, noticing Wistman's Wood in the distance, on the left. A detour can be made on the other side of the stile, following the newtake wall up to Crockern Tor and then returning to the path leading to the wood.

At Crockern Tor, with its slablike rocks, it needs only a touch of imagination to picture the Stannary Parliament of the old tinning industry that was once held here. Parliament

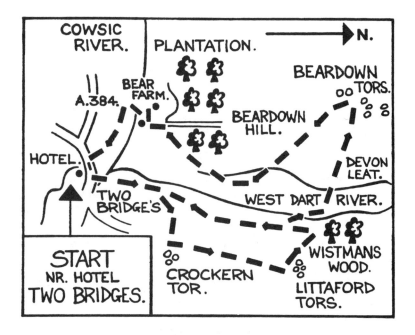

COWSIC RIVER. PLANTATION. N.

BEARDOWN TORS.

BEAR FARM.
A.384.

BEARDOWN HILL.

DEVON LEAT.

HOTEL.

WEST DART RIVER.

TWO BRIDGE'S.

WISTMANS WOOD.

START
NR. HOTEL
TWO BRIDGES.

CROCKERN TOR.

LITTAFORD TORS.

Rock and Court Floor tell their own story. The view from here is beautiful, with south-eastern Dartmoor spreading itself around, and the road below running along to distant Princetown.

Littaford Tors stand high on the ridge, to the left of Crockern Tor, and in this vicinity are the remains of a prehistoric enclosure and hut circles. Other hut circles are scattered on each side of the West Dart river, winding along at the bottom of the slope.

Wistman's Wood is a Nature Conservancy Forest Nature Reserve, one of three areas of oakwood growing at a high altitude on Dartmoor. A cluster of enormous stones protects the dwarfed trees, producing a rich growth of mosses and lichens. The word Wistman, it seems, has alternative derivations − it can either mean stony wood by water, or wood of the Celts.

In the central grove of the wood is an inscribed stone, marking the felling of a young oak by Wentworth Buller in

1866 in the name of scientific research. It was discovered that, by counting the rings of the tree, it could be aged to some 500 years.

(A) The shorter loop returns to Two Bridges picking a way along the sometimes wet ground beside the river. If the track becomes hazardous, the walker is advised to climb to the left, where a path can be found on dry turf. Wheatears and meadow pipits abound here.

(B) The longer walk continues through the wood, or above or below it, eventually crossing the river just below the weir, where a Water Authority building stands. The rough, steep side of Beardown presents quite a challenge if you attempt to cross before reaching the weir. There are great circles of bog, vivid with moss and rush. The flora is interesting, with stunted gorse bushes and small patches of heather and whortleberry. Overhead buzzards soar, ravens too, and perhaps a heron flaps heavily down the stream. It doesn't need much imagination to conjure up Bronze Age ladies rinsing out their smalls in the river below.

Halfway up the slope the Devenport Leat loops around the contours, a footpath accompanying it. Another pleasant detour offers itself here − a scramble uphill to explore Beardown Tor, where wonderful views of the moor stretching as far as the eye can see are a reward for aching legs after the hard climb.

The return walk to Two Bridges, however, is pleasantly easy, following the footpath beside the leat. Very soon a stile continues the path into the darkness of a stand of conifers. Watch for small brown trout in the waters of the leat. Another stile, and the view throws up North Hessary Tor, right in front of you. Two Bridges is just ahead with the hazy line of the south moors in the distance.

At the entrance to Beardown Farm the path is signed clearly, taking us through the yard and down a track, over Cowsic Bridge. Look back here, to the right, and see the restored clapper bridge upstream.

Follow the path, and the river, through a very beautiful

valley; the beech trees here suffered very badly in recent gales but the Cowsic river splashes and leaps among vast boulders, ignoring the carnage as it does so.

The path emerges on the main road and you are advised to cross − extremely carefully − and return to the car park via the old bridge. Walk in front of the hotel, originally called The Saracen's Head, and again cross back to the quarry and the waiting car.

Fernworthy Forest

A loop walk of 6-7 miles around the outside of the Forest, with added detours, and several waymarked walks within the Forest.

Fernworthy Forest, planted around a reservoir, is some 3 miles from Chagford, one of Dartmoor's ancient Stannary Towns where tin was stamped and coined in medieval times. Chagford may be reached by road from Exeter, via Whiddon Down or from Moretonhampstead.

For this walk, as for walk 14, it is important to be aware of activity on the three firing ranges on Dartmoor. Walkers are advised to seek day to day information before they plan their walks, from police stations, information centres and post offices, or by ringing direct to The Range Liaison Officer, DEVCOR Training Areas, Seaton Barracks, Tavistock Road, Plymouth, Tel: Plymouth 772312, extension 249.

At all times, watch out for red lights and flags warning of Ministry of Defence artillery and rifle practice. There is no firing in August, but it continues throughout the remainder of the year including some weekends.

This loop walk starts just inside the cattle grid at the entrance to the forest, where cars may be parked on the verge. Fernworthy Reservoir lies to the north and north west of this point, and the starting place for the actual forest walks is signed to the right 100yds inside the entrance.

The 6 mile loop lies outside the forest perimeter to begin with, hugging the edge and following the conifers around. Before the trees were planted, this was a bare sweep of moorland. In the 17th century the three farmsteads here

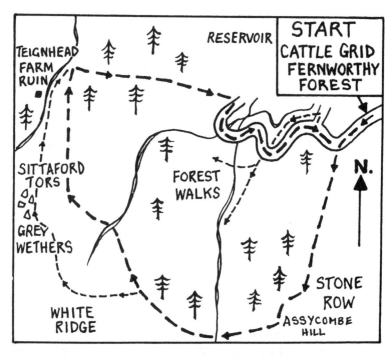

were referred to as a village. And back in the Bronze Age it was the home of the first Dartmoor settlers. The remains of their civilisation − cairns, hut circles, stone rows and burial places − still litter the moor, some of them lying within the forest bounds and visible when following the forest waymarked walks.

This trek beside the trees produces a variety of views as it heads due south, then south west and, turning the corner, abruptly north west and into the teeth of the wind, if it's that sort of weather. The ground is extremely boggy, particularly where small streams flow into the forest.

Having ascended and then left Assycombe Hill, negotiated the wet tussocks at the tip of the forest and then laboriously climbed White Ridge, we descend to a ford close by an entrance to the forest. Hut circles and pounds can be explored in the immediate vicinity, and are marked on the Ordnance Survey map.

Here an obvious path strikes out due west and upwards, taking us to the ridge, in the middle of which stand the two stone circles known as the Grey Wethers. These were undoubtedly erected as part of their religious rites by the early settlers, but little is known of their exact purpose. Another track crosses the circles heading due south and to Postbridge, not far away.

Above the Grey Wethers is Sittaford Tor − a climb that is steep and rough because of the tussocky ground, but the view from the summit is magnificent, with all the familiar peaks of Dartmoor laid out around us.

Old Teignhead farm, sheltered by its clump of trees, lies to the north just below the tor, with the baby North Teign river flashing and shining as it meanders through the valley below the farm. Built at the end of the 18th century, Teignhead (now a ruin), was once a thriving farmstead with solid outhouses, the warm, low-ceilinged kitchen the hub of family life. Farm carts rolled noisily over the stone bridge across the river. The place has long been derelict, stones lying untidily around the bare bones of the old house, the only signs of life the clusters of sheep and ponies cropping the turf that increasingly encroaches on what was once a home. It's worth making a detour across the clapper bridge to explore this old ruin.

Beyond the farm the northern moors curve away into the distance, with their desolate peat bogs and attendant firing range notices. Famous Cranmere Pool, the so-called heart of the moor, lies within these bogs. It is dangerous and illegal to enter land within the firing range when red flags − at night, red lights − are showing. Times of firing can be ascertained from local post offices and police stations or the Range Liaison Officer.

Opposite Teignhead farm is the forest entrance that will return this walk to the starting point. The bridlepath is downhill and easy. Various firebreaks and other forestry paths make it simple to explore among the trees for Bronze Age antiquities. The path ends at a gate close to the reservoir edge, from where a road returns to the parked car. The way down from the moor, through the forest, can be a strange experience − from the vastness of Dartmoor we step into the quiet, shadowed path between the trees, with the light making strange patterns down the maze of tunnels and firebreaks. Leaving the forest finally is like shutting the door of a dark house; such contrast makes for a memorable walking experience.

In the summer season − starting at Easter − leaflets describing walks waymarked in the forest are available for walkers. These are free and can be found in the small car park signed 'Reservoir and Forest Walks, Park and WCs' on the right of the road as you enter the forest. Walks are signed by posts with coloured tops − follow the colour of your choice and refer to the leaflet for description of route and places of interest. In particular, search out the remains of early habitation now revealed by clear-felling around the Assycombe area.

The Teign Gorge

A loop walk of 4½ miles, with a possible added detour of 2 miles.

The river Teign runs between the steep, tree-clad slopes of the gorge just a mile due south of the picturesque Dartmoor village of Drewsteignton, providing excellent walking, both on the heights of the gorge and along the riverside below. This is romantic, evocative countryside, and the footpaths afford a wealth of possible loop walks and leisurely explorations.

The start of the walk is very nearly 1 mile from Sandy Park (north east of Chagford) along the Drewsteignton road, which is also signed Castle Drogo. Cars may be parked on the right-hand verge of this road.

A footpath sign indicates Hunter's Path and Fisherman's Path, and we cross the cattle grid at the entrance to Gibhouse and Coombe Farm. Beside some old beech trees take the path signed 'Hunter's Path', going though a gate and heading left and upwards.

Castle Drogo, above, was built between 1910 and 1930 and designed by Sir Edwin Lutyens. Now acquired by the National Trust, it is open to the public daily, except on Fridays, from the beginning of April to the end of October. The castle hides itself behind a sparse fringe of pine trees as it looks down into the wooded gorge, 900 ft below.

Along our way there are two stepped paths on the left, signed 'Castle Drogo and Gardens'. Occasional seats are provided on which to rest and enjoy the view. From the summit of Hunter's Tor it's possible to see some unaccustomed views of Dartmoor's humps and bumps.

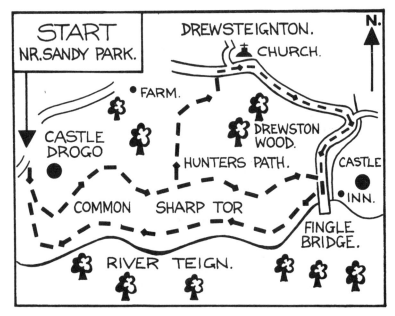

Follow this path around the horseshoe bends, with the ground falling gradually away on the right to the depths of the gorge. Far below the sun occasionally strikes a glint of water, and sometimes pin-people may be seen making their way along the lower Fisherman's Path − our own route back.

The initials MW on footpath signs stand for Two Moors Way, some 102 miles of rural footpaths stretching from Lynmouth on the North Devon coast to Ivybridge in South Devon. These paths were originally walked by mariners, monks, travelling preachers, farmers and miners − this heritage of access is a precious one.

The loop detour of 2 miles begins further along the Hunter's Path, where a signed path runs sharply off to the left, climbing uphill among the bracken fronds. This leads to Drewsteignton. It crosses fields and woodland, heading north, eventually joining a well-used footpath between high hedges and emerging at the entrance to the village. Here it's enjoyable to loiter for a while, admiring the lovely old granite cottages and the sombre beauty of the grey church. The

Drewe Arms remains a typical Dartmoor inn of olden days, evoking the simple, hard life that people lived then. A mile-long, downhill road leads out of the village, signed to Fingle Bridge, where it joins up with the end of the Hunter's Path as it comes out onto the road just above the bridge.

But, ignoring the detour to Drewsteignton, the Hunter's Path continues on its dizzy course, going to Fingle by way of a right-hand fork signed to Fingle Bridge. Down we go. This path joins the road close to the car park of the Angler's Rest Free House and Restaurant, where excellent refreshments of all varieties are offered, guaranteed to tickle the palate of the most jaded walker. It is open for normal licensing hours during the spring and summer, but from the end of September and during the winter only as follows – Monday to Friday from 11 am to 2.30 pm, Saturday 11 am to 2.30 pm and from 7 pm, Sunday from 12.30 pm to 2.30 pm.

On the site of the Angler's Rest there was originally an old mill. Here the accommodating miller built a 'parlour' and a kitchen, where visiting travellers were allowed to prepare their own provisions. After the mill, a teahouse run by two Victorian ladies occupied the site. There are some interesting old pictures inside the Angler's Rest which show not only the tea house, but the original mill. Fingle Bridge is alive with history.

It is also a wonderful haven for flora and fauna. In spring salmon struggle upstream, urgent in their need to return to their spawning grounds, leaping over weirs and obstacles on the way. A huge variety of woodland and riverside birds feed, nest and breed here. Watch out for the small, white bib-fronted dipper, bobbing on a water-bound boulder before diving down to walk on the river bed in search of grubs and nymphs from under the stones. Bluebells, campion, heather and bracken, all take their turn in adorning the changing seasons, and the fiery colours of dying leaves in autumn contain all the tones of an artist's palette.

Across the old bridge, built in the 16th century to take

packhorses on their weary way to market, there is an area of woodland. Here again footpaths abound. The zig-zag route up to Cranbrooke Castle may not be everybody's cup of tea on a hot day, but the view at the end of it, when the rough-clad ramparts are reached, a thousand feet above the river, is reward enough for the demanding climb. Close to the upward path lies a simple wooden cross — all that remains of a Cavalier's grave, a reminder of the Civil War when many skirmishes were fought up and down the river Teign.

The entrance to the river path — our way back — is opposite the Angler's Rest entrance, and is signed Fisherman's Path, Dogmarsh Bridge and Chagford, and the road near Castle Drogo. Here the National Trust has established a secure path slightly above the river bank level. It is possible to walk closer to the water, but slippery boulders and intrusive roots are a hazard. The new path is safer, even though at one point there are some perilous steps which this particular walker negotiated on all fours, having no head for precipitous, unguarded sides.

Just beyond the little weir, notice the specially constructed salmon-leaps. The path divides at the next sign, Chagford being to the left and our way taking us up beside Gibhouse and then back to the starting place.

Buckfastleigh

A loop walk of 5 miles, with an extra 2 miles if wished, over hilly moorland with breathtaking scenery.

Buckfast Abbey, founded and endowed by Canute, is the centrepiece of the village of Buckfastleigh, sprawled around the busy A38(T) road between Ashburton and South Brent. Its environs, on the south east fringe of Dartmoor, provide excellent walking. There are several pubs and at least one café in Buckfastleigh.

Take the Bussell Road — signed 'Town Hall' — out of Buckfastleigh, and drive westward to Cross Furzes. Here cars may be left on the road verges. A bridlepath is signed to Moor Cross 2 miles, South Brent 4¾, and waymarked blue. The Abbots' Way is signed Plym Ford 7 miles, and Nuns Cross for Princetown, 10 miles. Following these signs, take the path which crosses Dean Burn at a small clapper bridge, dated 1972 when restoration took place. Go through the gate, following the orange square, which changes to blue waymarks as the track continues, leading on to Water Oak Corner, having crossed Lambs Down.

The ancient track known as the Abbots' Way was a 'post road' travelled by the old Cistercian monks, who were wool traders, when taking their wares to Plymouth. It was a useful path linking Buckfast Abbey with Buckland Abbey in south west Dartmoor.

The track crosses Brockhill Ford, which feeds into the Avon Dam Reservoir nearby, and follows the Abbots' Way as it runs beside the Avon river, heading upstream.

All around are the remains of tin mining, the slag heaps and diggings now returned to their original green turf. If one

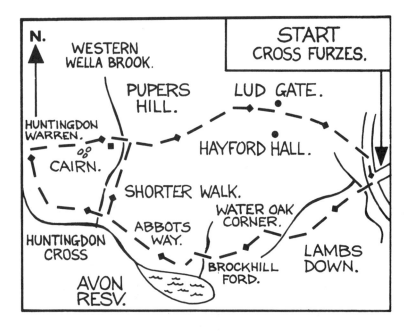

could have a bird's eye view, the tinning scars would appear as a fish's skeleton; the stream is the backbone, the lateral bones revealing the workings of tin lodes reaching out into the surrounding moorland.

All that remains of a stoned enclosure can be seen below the summit of the hill on the right — Hickaton Hill. Tin miners were the last in a long line of men who lived and worked in these bleak hills and valleys. There are, in fact, three pounds on the hillside nearby, and another below the surface of the dam. Hut circles, too, trace forgotten lines of homesteads, now eroded and overgrown.

The expanse of moorland on the opposite side of the Avon river is covered in bracken. Bishops Mead's elegant shape complements the lines of other hills below the dam. At this point we stand in the middle of enclosed moorland — a precious moment. Looking ahead we can see the contours of the Avon and, on the skyline, the triangular Redlake clay-tip, a relic of former workings.

At the confluence of the Wallabrook with the Avon stands Huntingdon Cross, part of the Two Moors Way, and known to have been in situ in 1557.

(A) If the longer loop is being followed, the Wallabrook can be negotiated − with care in winter − by stepping stones. This continues on among the humps and bumps of slag heaps, beside the Avon, keeping left of a large patch of rushes, until it reaches the clapper bridge about ½ mile upstream. This is a beautiful path, winding between pockets of wetland and sheltered from the wind which is normally a feature of this walk.

The clapper bridge is a good point for picnicking among boulders by the waterside. On the opposite side of the river the Abbots' Way continues on towards distant Princetown, but our way takes us upriver on the same side, passing spectacular Broad Falls and pausing to look for the remains of a blowing house nearby. It is not difficult to imagine how water was diverted by leat to power the machinery necessary to convert tin ore into ingots. These were then carried by pony back to the market towns. Now only the scars among heather and turf, with piles of littered stones protruding, remain as an indication of a past vital industry.

The Avon continues up to Avon Head, rising somewhere in the folds of the far hills, but we turn east, following a deep gulley and climbing steadily through rough moorland until the summit of Huntingdon Barrow is reached, and the cairn called the Heap o' Sinners. Pause here for breath, and to add the traditional stone to the cairn.

The way back is downhill, descending due east from the cairn and passing through the ruins of Warren House, where a farmstead existed before the close of the 17th century. This path joins up with the shorter loop as it returns, via Lud Gate, to Cross Furzes.

(B) For the shorter walk stay this side of the Wallabrook, following it north-eastwards and exploring the many mining relics that litter the moorland. Watch out for pit holes and overgrown gulleys of the old workings. The pits are deep,

open and treacherous, but there is much to be seen, particularly the big wheelpit, where the remaining stones stand out clearly amidst the surrounding debris. Just beyond the wheelpit look for the remains of a tiny church, built in 1909 by the Reverend Keble Martin and his friends. The writer of the *Concise British Flora in Colour* was a regular visitor to this area.

To the west, the ruin of Warren House on the hillside is a reminder of the past when rabbits were brought over from Europe by the Normans. Although meant for sport, they were also bred to provide welcome food for the tin miners living in such remote parts of the moor. Warrens were controlled by a warrener living nearby — this ruin belonged to such a one. Difficult now to visualise it as a sturdy homestead, with a charming garden, as related by Eric Hemery in his masterpiece, *High Dartmoor*.

The path bears east and then north east, joining a clear track down towards Lud Gate, one of the oldest moorland gates, and at this point — near the remains of Warren House — picking up the longer loop detailed above. From Lud Gate a mile long lane returns us to Cross Furzes.

Powderham and Kenton

A 3¼ mile loop walk, with an addition of a 2 mile riverside walk.

Kenton, the home of Powderham Castle, is a small village on the busy A379 coast road from Exeter to Newton Abbot. Cars may be left in the free car park beside the small triangle of grass enclosing the war memorial.

There are no cafes in the village, but the general store sells soft drinks in bottles and a variety of groceries. The Devon Arms and the Dolphin Inn offer refreshment in licensing hours.

This walk, although beginning along the busy main road, soon turns off through footpaths into a quiet country road and also, if desired, extends the route for 2 extra miles along the river Exe.

Leaving the war memorial, turn right and follow the A379 for nearly ½ mile, passing the entrance to Powderham Castle. This small, but captivating stately home is open to the public daily, except on Fridays and Saturdays, from 27th May to 13th September, 2 pm to 5 pm.

A little further along the road, opposite Old Jail House in the part of the village called Southtown, a footpath will be seen entering the castle grounds by a stile. This path crosses the meadow in the direction it is signed, continuing left after going through an iron gate and then turning sharp right at the end of the field. Continue, with the river Kenn on your left, until the path emerges into the road beside the river Exe. Turn left here.

This pleasant road meanders along beside the wide river, with Powderham Castle and its magnificent deer park on the

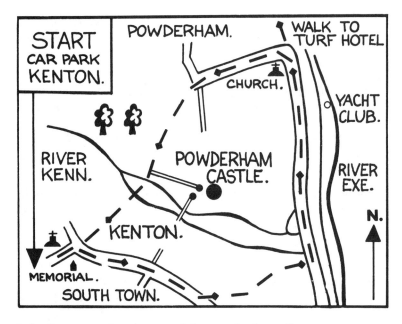

left. Between the river and the road, the railway runs past, with a view of the old pumping house at Starcross behind us, a memory of Brunel's Atmospheric Railway. In winter and wet weather this road is sometimes flooded, but on a fine day it provides easy walking with splendid views all around.

On the opposite side of the river Exe, Lympstone is a picturesque huddle between redstone cliffs, while Exmouth's grey, spreading sprawl reaches down to the sea at the river mouth.

At low tide the bird life on the mudflats of the estuary is enormously varied. Solitary herons may often be seen fishing the streams in the deer park, or roosting in the trees — there is an old-established heronry here — and the castle herd of fallow deer wander at will beneath the huge trees. The castle itself can be glimpsed from this road, a small, squat building that contains its medieval origins within restored walls.

The road passes Starcross Yacht Club and, opposite, a grown-over secret entrance to the castle grounds that must often have been used when Fairfax's Roundheads besieged the castle in 1645. Where the road turns sharply left, beside the church, a footpath on the right signs the way to the riverside walk, *a detour of 2 miles* which crosses the railway line − watch out and listen for trains − and follows the river up to the Turf Hotel and the beginning of the Exeter Canal. Built in 1566, this canal was made to resolve the problem of the weir thrown across the river by the Countess of Devon, who was displeased with the citizens of Exeter and thus hoped to stop their trading facilities. With the advent of this, the first lock canal in the country, Exeter was once again made accessible to shipping and trade.

Bird watchers really come into their own on this added walk, and, if timed for low tide, it is very exciting to watch the birds coming down to their feeding grounds. Ducks, geese, curlew and oyster catchers fill the air with their voices, and the river becomes full of churning wings. Beyond the Turf Hotel, where excellent bar food is available, footpaths lead on to Exeter, but although a track leads across the railway line in the direction of Powderham, this is a private road and does *not* grant access to walkers. We must, therefore, retrace our steps to the road that now turns right towards Powderham church and the loop that will take us back to Kenton.

Powderham church is made of red sandstone and is listed as one of the treasures of England. It is full of memories of long-dead Courtenays, and crowned by a medieval weathervane in the shape of a dolphin. The enormous oak trees that shade the church entrance have yielded up cannon balls, relics of the Civil War when both castle and church were under fire.

Passing the church, the long tree-lined avenue leads up towards another entrance to the castle, beside some attractive pink-washed cottages. Three great cork oaks dominate the entrance area.

On the hill facing us stands an old belvedere, whose all-seeing eye rakes the river and the hills beyond. With the castle entrance on our left, we take the signed footpath that runs up the side of the field beneath the belvedere, towards a ridge of woodland. Beside the trees the path descends again, with the deer park on its left. Here, on a hot day, the deer often graze in the shade of the superb old trees, seeming not to notice admiring walkers. There are some immense sweet chestnuts along this path, with twisted boles and limbs. Wild flowers, laurel and rhododendron edge our way. With peeps of the castle to our left, we seem to be back in the more leisured, pastoral past.

Leaving the woodland, the path takes us down steps to water meadows where cattle often graze. A bridge crosses the little river Kenn and eventually we reach the fringe of a housing estate. The clear path emerges through a gate near the Old Bakehouse. A few more steps and we are in Fore Street, Kenton, just opposite the war memorial and the parked car.

Teignmouth to Dawlish

A 5 mile walk, with an alternative loop of 4½ miles, or shorter loop of 3½ miles, which includes return from Dawlish by bus.

Teignmouth can be reached by the A379 road from Exeter or by train or by bus from Exeter or Torquay. The seawall is the starting point of this walk, which encompasses both flat and hilly walking on country roads, footpaths and farm tracks, with an alternative bus ride back from Dawlish if required. Pay car parks are numerous in Teignmouth, as are hotels, pubs and tea houses.

The seawall leads us towards Dawlish, and runs alongside Isambard Kingdom Brunel's famous railway, the line that revolutionised tourist traffic to the West Country. Completed in 1847, it was called the Atmospheric Railway as it made use of air pressure to propel trains at a maximum speed of 64 miles an hour. 'Silent Speed' was a Victorian venture which failed ultimately through lack of finance. Pumping stations were built at regular intervals along the track, and one such tower still stands today on the far side of Dawlish, at Starcross Station.

The walk along the seawall is extremely pleasant, with sheltering red sandstone cliffs above, swathed in greenery and wild flowers, and a variety of bird life to watch when the tide is right.

At certain conditions of low tide there is the opportunity of searching the surface of the beach for traces of the salt pans which were the source of Teignmouth's first industrial venture, far back in history.

The little triangle of rock and land known as Sprey Point

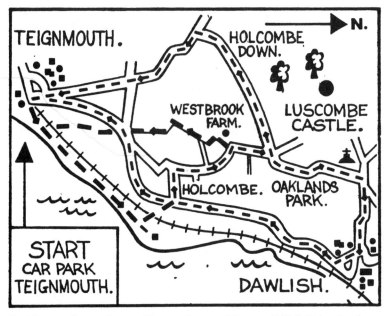

halfway along the wall was formed by a cliff fall in the last century. Sixty years ago a tea house stood here. On a clear day there is a good view, from the Ore Stone off the furthermost point to the east, to Portland in the west, looking out to sea.

The end of the seawall falls short of a famous rock formation called The Parson and The Clerk, which, legend tells us, is all that was left of a Dawlish vicar and his clerk who dared to defy the Devil. Even more striking is Shag Rock, usually crowned with sea birds. Steps lead from the wall into Smuggler's Cove, but don't attempt this at high tide. The echoes of history resonate all around here, as you pass beneath the railway and climb the steep and narrow Smuggler's Lane.

The main road to Exeter streams past here, a very dangerous crossing, and the opposite, quieter road leads into the old-world village of Holcombe. A little way up the hill turn right and climb up to the Castle Inn for timely refreshment, if required. A peaceful country lane winds on through well-wooded banks from here and passes Westbrook Farm. Here a decision must be made whether to return to Teignmouth by bus or on foot.

If a bus ride is decided on, climb the hill past the farm and then turn right down Oak Hill to the parish church of St Gregory in the neighbouring village of Dawlish. It is worth making a detour through the churchyard and the old glebe lands of Newhay, where the spirit of rural Dawlish lives on. To finish this loop, follow the river through Dawlish's Manor Gardens and Strand Gardens, until the sea front is reached, when a bus can be caught back to Teignmouth.

Alternatively, the walk may be completed on foot, by turning left at the junction of Oak Hill and Holcombe Down Road, and following this latter road along a tree-lined ridge which affords magnificent views on each side. Turn left at the T-junction at its end. Here we descend, via a steep, rough, but metalled road into a pleasant housing estate, and so down to the junction of New Road and Woodway Road in Teignmouth. By following Woodway Road straight down hill, we join the main Exeter Road and can reach the seawall − our point of departure − by crossing the large car and coach park on the left of this road, some hundred yards above the church of St Michael on the seafront.

The last alternative, which completes the 5 mile version of this walk, is to turn in at the entrance to Westbrook Farm on the road out of Holcombe − no footpath sign here − cross the ford, and then follow the rough path which is flinty, steep and very muddy in bad weather, veering left and upward. This eventually joins a larger track coming in from the left. Continue, keeping left at the next fork. This is pleasant walking, along a grassy once-metalled road, with sea views on the left. Go down the hill, passing farm outbuildings, where the going is marshy after rain, and then uphill, finally emerging in the Teignmouth fringe of Holcombe village at Oak Hill Cross Road by Turnpike Cottage, originally a toll house.

Cross the road here − again, a dangerous crossing − and

then follow Cliff Road, which is a quiet footpath running down to Teignmouth via the railway bridge, close to where the seawall begins. A footpath sign indicates this track.

One other diversion is to turn right, after a kissing gate, into fields signed 'Public Gardens', and follow, left and downward, to the railway bridge. This little path runs parallel with the grounds of Cliffden, originally one of the rich and ancient mansions in Teignmouth, now a privately owned holiday hotel for the blind. Where the path emerges onto the railway bridge, a handsome entrance supports a stone dated 1887.

Just before the start of the seawall is a raised walkway once called 'Old Maid's Walk', the shelters being built in 1935 to celebrate King George V's Silver Jubilee. The promenade sweeps down to the river mouth, with the red sandstone, tree-covered prominence called The Ness on the opposite shore. Teignmouth Pier was once intact and much used; built in the 1860s, Victorian and, later, Edwardian concerts, dances and steamer trips established its popularity. Now its sad and neglected remains are offensive to the eye. Perhaps the new age of leisure will eventually rebuild it, bringing back to Teignmouth promenade all the gaiety and fun of its earlier existence.

The River Teign Estuary

A loop walk of 4 miles plus an additional, optional loop of 2½ miles.

The estuary of the river Teign has attractive, fairly unfrequented country on its southern banks, and provides interesting walking for those who like something a little out of the ordinary. Attention must be paid to tide tables, and it is advisable to wait until at least one hour after high tide before starting this walk along the river beach. Even in summer there is plenty of mud and wet sand, so shoes must be strong and waterproof. DO NOT walk when the tide is coming in.

A good point to start either of these two loop walks is at Arch Brook Bridge, 1½ miles due west of the small village of Ringmore, an extension of Shaldon, which lies on the opposite bank of the river to Teignmouth, at the mouth of the estuary. There is a regular bus service from Teignmouth to Newton Abbot via Shaldon which will drop passengers at Arch Brook Bridge.

Here the river comes slightly inland to form a small creek and there is a car park for walkers who wish to sample all, or part of, The Templer Way, an approximately 20 mile long walk which is detailed on the notice board in the car park. Our way follows this route for the next 1¾ miles, with wheelchair waymarks indicating the path.

The first loop of the walk follows the footpath that hugs the river bank going upstream towards Newton Abbot, beneath shady old trees growing out of the redstone cliffs. Wading birds, herons and seagulls haunt these muddy

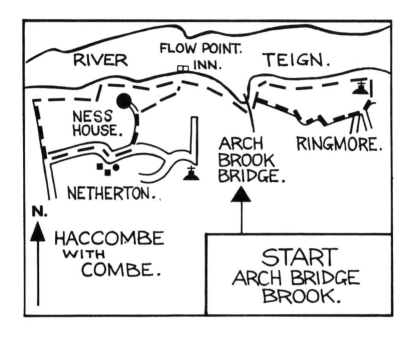

reaches of the Teign, and the air is alive with bird sound. On the day of walking, we heard the piping alarm cries of redshank and saw oyster catchers, shelduck and black-headed gulls, as well as − further up the river − a small group of beautifully crested mergansers, a real mark-up for dedicated bird-watchers. Note the huge retaining wall about 100 metres along the bank, built no doubt as a result of flooding and erosion. On a day when the wind blows from the south west you will feel it slapping your face as you walk up-river.

Quite soon Coombe Cellars Inn comes into sight, against a magnificent back-drop of three famous Dartmoor peaks − Hay Tor on the right, with Saddle Tor and then Rippon Tor stretching left along the skyline. Coombe Cellars, once a row of primitive fishermen's cottages, with a long history of smuggling, has a superb restaurant and very good bar food during licensing hours.

Turn left up the slipway just below the inn and then right, into the car park, where the footpath sign indicates the way along a pavemented path, following the line of the river and passing a children's play area. Continue along this path beyond the inn, enjoying the view up and down river. Almost opposite is the village of Bishopsteignton, with Haldon Moor above. Buckingham Palace is the name of a rock on the river bank below Bishopsteignton where, legend says, a crazy old man lived for many years. Just beyond the inn, a footpath sign faces a field beside the river − note that this is the exit point of our return loop walk.

As a matter of interest, the way ahead becomes quite rough, and must set a great challenge to any wheelchair ramblers who are determined to continue.

At Netherton Point − recognisable by its flat spread of grass and ensuing inlet − we turn left, heading towards the top of the creek, then again follow the waterline. Here, when the tide is low, bird-lovers will again find plenty to see. Hundreds of gulls and waders of all sorts lined the opposite bank of the Teign on our day of walking, and many cormorants hung out their wings to dry.

Just before reaching the sewage works at Buckland Point, turn left up a rough track, now disregarding the wheelchair route which continues along the beach towards distant Newton Abbot. This is the start of our return journey. Follow this steep and muddy path, a typical example of a Devon sunken lane which must have been used by local smugglers in past centuries, and notice the lush growth of hart's tongue ferns, violets, pennywort and many other native plants which line its banks. There are occasional gateways with tantalising glimpses of distant views on the way up − ideal places for catching one's breath!

Turn sharp left at the top of the lane and follow the road as it winds and bends through the ancient hamlet of Lower

Netherton, full of eye-catching old farmhouses and cottages, one of them still boasting an original oak-panelled door.

This is quite a muscular walk, with a steep hill leading out of the hamlet. On the level again, turn left at the cross-roads, where there is a cul-de-sac sign, taking the minor road leading to Netherton House. A short distance along this road a footpath sign on the right-hand side points the way back to Coombe Cellars Inn through the fields. Once through the gate, turn left, pass another gate and turn right, following the hedge and then walking down the middle of the next field to the footpath exit noticed earlier. From here take the river path back to Arch Brook.

A second loop from Arch Brook may be walked in the opposite direction to Ringmore. It is only fair to warn walkers that the return route is along an unpavemented country road, though it is possible to simply retrace one's footsteps on the river path, from Ringmore to Arch Brook Bridge.

The river path heads towards Shaldon, at the top of the estuary. Look out for a disused lime kiln hidden in the rocky cliffs that overshadow the beach − the story goes that a purse of gold is hidden within, only to be found by one who visits the place alone at midnight . . .

Reaching Ringmore, turn right and visit the tucked-away church of St Nicholas, which has a leper window close to the altar, a magnificent sundial on the wall adjoining the porch and, rather strangely, a small courtyard decorated with pebbled signs of the zodiac.

Should you decide not to retrace your steps but to brave the road walk back to Arch Brook, you will pass some attractive old houses, one with a beautiful circular leaded window, a large holiday camp along the way, and the tiny community of ancient buildings known as Old Teignharvey and Little Harvey Farmhouse, pink-washed and picturesquely thatched.

These two walks are especially attractive on a hot

summer day, when the cool serenity of the river Teign is a solace to both body and mind.

Acknowledgements and bibliography

I wish to acknowledge the help of the Dartmoor National Park Authority for information in many spheres, together with several of their publications; also the following authors, whose books have given me so much fascinating historical and topographical detail.

Dartmoor National Park, Official Guide. Edited John Weir, Michael Joseph, 1987.

Dartmoor National Park Walks 4, Haytor and Area. Christine Franklin, Edited by Elizabeth Prince, 1985.

Prehistoric Dartmoor. Paul Pettit, David & Charles, 1974.

Dartmoor Mines, The Mines of the Granite Mass. Michael Atkinson with Roger Burt and Peter Waite, Exeter Industrial Archaeology Group, Dept. of Economic History, University of Exeter, 1978.

Guide to Dartmoor. William Crossing, David & Charles, 1965.

Devon (A New Survey of England). W.G. Hoskins, Collins, 1954.

The Haytor Granite Tramway and Stover Canal. M.C. Ewans, David & Charles, 1966.

The Templer Way. Derek Beavis, Obelisk Publications, 1992.

High Dartmoor, Land and People. Eric Hemery, Robert Hale, London, 1983.

The Witchcraft and Folklore of Dartmoor. Ruth St Leger-Gordon, Alan Sutton Publishing Ltd, 1982.